Co-creating with God

Learn how to let your creativity loose in every area of life.

Lyn Packer

Co-creating with God

CO-CREATING WITH GOD

Copyright © 2017 Lyn Packer

All rights reserved. No part of this book may be reproduced in any form, by any means without the express permission of the author. This includes reprints, photocopying, recording, or any future means of reproducing text.

Bible and Concordance versions used in this book

NASB – Unless otherwise indicated, Scripture quotations taken from the NEW AMERICAN STANDARD BIBLE®(NASB), Copyright © 1960, 1962, 1963, 1968, 1971, 1972, 1973, 1975, 1977, 1995 by The Lockman Foundation, Used by permission. www.Lockman.org"

KJV – King James Version – The Holy Bible, KING JAMES VERSION. Cambridge Edition: 1769; King James Bible Online, 2017.

NIV – New International Version – THE HOLY BIBLE, NEW INTERNATIONAL VERSION®, NIV® Copyright © 1973, 1978, 1984, 2011 by Biblica, Inc.® Used by permission. All rights reserved worldwide.

ESV – The Holy Bible, English Standard Version. ESV® Permanent Text Edition® (2016). Copyright © 2001 by Crossway Bibles, a publishing ministry of Good News Publishers.

Concordance references used in this book are taken from Strongs Concordance – Strong, James. STRONG'S EXHAUSTIVE CONCORDANCE OF THE BIBLE. Abingdon Press, 1890.

Published by:
XP Publishing
A Department of Patricia King Ministries
PO Box 1017
Maricopa, AZ 85139

ISBN: 1-378-62166-328-7

Endorsements

Lyn Packer's life is the life of an unrestricted creator! Her imagination and curiosity have been unleashed as a lifestyle that has been blessing lives internationally for years. Across multiple disciplines Lyn creates with excellence and life-transforming significance as she infuses the heart of God into her passions. Lyn's new book, *Co-Creating with God*, has captured decades of profound training on creativity and is guaranteed to encourage, inspire and unleash the creative potential within you! Whether you think you have zero creativity or you are a pro, *Co-creating with God* will awaken the exhilaration of creating in seamless union with Heaven.

> BENJI ALEXANDER, DIRECTOR
> REVIVAL SCHOOL AOTEAROA
> NEW ZEALAND

While I've had decades of exposure to books and manuals on creativity, including those coming from a biblical perspective, Lyn Packer's *Co-creating with God* is one of the most accessible, inspiring and practical tools I've encountered. Not only does Lyn dispel two common lies that self-proclaimed noncreatives believe, "I'm not creative," and "Even if I am, it's too late," but she provides easy, applicable exercises to explore and express that creativity which, for many, has been buried deep inside for decades. And for those who already heartily embrace our creative natures, Lyn has given us a guide to further hone our abilities, as well as use them, while leading others on their own journeys of discovery. *Co-creating with God* is a resource I'll be recommending and turning to for ideas and inspiration again and again.

MELISSA WILLIAMS-POPE
WRITER, ACTOR, SINGER AND SUCCESS COACH FOR
WOMEN ENTREPRENEURS
WWW.MELISSAWILLIAMSPOPE.COM

In *Co-creating with God*, Lyn Packer has dipped deep into her own creative genius and shared with us valuable tools to release and restore delight, joy, and breakthrough in our lives. She opens the hangar doors of your mind for essential "flights of imagination," slays some "creativity killers," and encourages you to join her on the adventure of a lifetime. Don't delay, read this book, get inspired and step boldly into living creatively in every area of your life. As she points out – it's never too late for creative exploits.

LYN LASNESKI
FOUNDER OF SCHOOL OF
CREATIVE GENIUS
VACAVILLE, CALIFORNIA, USA

Lyn is one of life's great mysteries. How one can be so gifted in so many different ways is truly baffling. Her depth of skill and creative anointing is second only to the depth of love and service towards others in her heart. Creativity is simply participating in our God-given divine nature as those who are made in the image and likeness of the Creator. When we create, we join in the likeness of our Father, participating in the divine nature. Lyn lives, breathes, and walks this divine life of participation. It's a joy to watch and learn from. We have received so much over the years

ENDORSEMENTS

from Lyn and we know our story would not be the same without her input. It is with great pleasure that I am able to wholeheartedly endorse both this book, *Co-creating with God*, and its writer.

> JOSH KLINKENBERG
> DIRECTOR INFLAME MINISTRIES
> SOUNDS OF THE NATIONS GLOBAL DIRECTOR

I am so glad Lyn has written this book! She has taught and brought this flow of creative teaching, accompanied by practical application, to our Revival School students for several years now. This has invariably connected people to the creative grace that so powerfully resides in all of us, and has also brought creativity out of us all, to a whole new light. We are creative beings, simply because we are created in God's image, who is the Master Creator. Psalm 139 talks about the creative process of our birth. Insights by the Master Creator of Him knitting us together (creative) intricately and curiously wrought as if embroidered with various colours (AMP). Wow! Such a picture of God's detailed, colour-full, creation of you. But most of us have this amazing creative part of our humanity constrained and ignored, mainly through mindset and ignorance. This book will help you unlock your creative birthright as a child of God. Creating stuff is just such a part of who we are, and such a source of joy and life. Don't be ripped off any longer. Fight for your birthright. *Co-creating with God* will bring you the understandings and the tools to win this fight. You are embroidered with various colours. So go colour your world.

> JOHN STEFFENS
> BUSINESS OWNER – AWARDED MNZM FOR HIS SERVICES TO NEW ZEALAND BUSINESS
> SENIOR PASTOR
> FIORDLAND NEW LIFE CHURCH

Reading through Lyn's book, *Co-creating with God*, at first my thoughts were, "This book is for others, not for me – I'm not an artistic sort of person." How wrong I was. From the opening pages, Lyn opened my eyes to see that I was a creative expression of a loving God. In loving Him and loving others, my own unique creatively could find expression within my divine design. What began as a simple read turned into an exciting journey. Being creative is no longer the expression of the gifted few, but the unveiling of who I want to be. Expect to find your concepts challenged and your creativity released as you read and experience the freedom contained within these pages.

>Pam Watson
>Senior Pastor
>Pursuit Church
>Auckland, New Zealand

Table of Contents

Introduction   11

How to Use This Book   13

1. What's So Important About Creativity?   19
2. God and Creativity   31
3. Imagine That   41
4. Losing Me, Finding Me   55
5. Oh, the Possibilities!   65
6. The Creative Process   75
7. Develop Your Creativity Further   83
8. Creativity in Later Life   95
9. Developing a Culture of Creativity   105
10. More Creativity Activators   115

Extra Features:

Bonus Chapter. The Value of Your Values   129

Scripture References On Creativity and Imagination   139

Study Guide Questions   155

Acknowledgments   165

About Lyn Packer   167

Introduction

A creative life is one where curiosity has been given permission to explore its world.

When God created mankind in His image, something was set in motion that continues to this day – the power of creativity was released. And it has continued to do its work, day in and day out, throughout the ages.

God spoke and His creative power went to work – light overtook darkness, order overcame chaos, worlds were created, life came into being, and mankind was created and inhabited the earth. Inventiveness was released into the world of mankind. Time passed, problems were solved, dominion was established and extended, languages were invented and communicated.

The power of creativity continues today in you. Whether you're a businessman, a shop assistant, a young mother or an 80-year-old grandfather, you can nurture, enhance, and increase your creativity. And creativity is not just confined to the arts; through this book you'll learn how to develop and bring your creativity into everything you do.

Do you long to be more creative than you presently are? Perhaps you think that creativity is confined to "those creative types." You may even think that you were "left on the shelf" when the creativity gene was handed out. If so, this book can definitely help you! You'll find life-stories, proven tips, training techniques and lots of activations that will help you develop and strengthen your creativity.

Come on a journey of discovery with me – see what God says about the creativity He has placed within you, and how you can explore it, develop it, and gain great satisfaction from it. Discover how it can be a blessing to you, giving you a more fulfilling and healthy life, and how it can also be a blessing to others as you use your creativity in God's service. Even if you think you're not creative, you'll discover that, in fact, you are. You'll discover ways you can explore and develop that creativity and then use your creativity to give you and others a better quality of life.

How to Use This Book
individually and as a study guide

*Don't let your life be defined by false boundary lines
that were never God's intention for you.*

Everyone benefits when their creativity is acknowledged, developed and released. In fact, research has proven that when that happens, measurable differences result in many areas – from an individual's health and wellbeing to community transformation.

As you read this book, you may find that you want to highlight passages or write notations in the margins of the pages. Feel free to do so; and I encourage you to do so creatively – use colored pens, or doodle meaningful pictures that illustrate what you were thinking at the time. But be aware that if you do, you probably won't want to lend the book to anyone else. I often find that I end up buying an extra copy of books I think I'll write in, so that I have my copy and one I can loan out.

The Creativity Activators

Throughout this book you'll find personal Creativity Activators at the end of each chapter that will awaken, activate, and strengthen your creativity. In order to fulfill some of the activations in this book, you'll need a few simple supplies which are mentioned in the Creativity Activators at the end of this chapter.

Each of the activations in this book will help expand and develop your creativity, and are there for specific purposes that will cause insight into your life and growth. Each time you do the activations you'll find that something different happens; you'll get new revelation and discover new things about your creativity.

How to use this book as a study guide

Co-creating with God provides a great opportunity to activate and promote creativity not only in you individually but in your church or community group as well. The activations included are ideal to get people to think about and use their creativity. This applies both to those reading the book on their own for personal growth and for those using it as a study guide in groups to help promote and develop creativity. In the back of the book you'll find some study questions for each chapter that you can use individually or discuss as a group. Using these questions will bring you to a greater place of understanding others and encouraging them in their creativity.

People often use existing groups, like home groups that are already set up, to facilitate a study of this sort. This book on creativity is a great study for all your home groups to do, as it's something everyone will gain great benefit from. If you would prefer to create a special interest group in order to facilitate this study, then that will work well, too.

HOW TO USE THIS BOOK

Group size – Keep your groups small; between 8 and 16 members is usually best. That's enough to still hold a discussion if several are absent, but not so many that discussions become unwieldy.

Frequency of meeting – I recommend once a week – I have found that to be best. More than that will not give people time to process what they've read on a personal level. If you meet less frequently, you will often run the risk of them forgetting to do the reading and activations during the intervening time.

Choose a group facilitator – someone who will oversee the discussion. You may already have this in place in a home group setting. A facilitator's role is to:

- Create a place where people feel free to take an active part in the group.

- Facilitate – not take over the meeting or take on the role of an expert. If they do so, it becomes more of a seminar and less of a group interacting with each other.

- Help the group adhere to agreed upon group expectations.

- Facilitate discussion, and see that quieter people are included while more vocal people don't monopolize discussion.

- Help the group stay on focus so the discussion doesn't wander off into unrelated topics.

Set out any group expectations or guidelines for involvement, such as:

- Bring your study guide (and Bible) with you each week to refer to during the meeting.

- Honour each other by coming regularly and on time.

- Do any assignments for the session.

- Come prepared to share – your input is important.

- Understand any expectations for healthy discussion. Discuss and come to agreement as a group on what expectations you have concerning this.

- Agree to disagree respectfully.

- Encourage one another; be open to different opinions and to having your ideas challenged.

- Stay on focus.

Have the group read one chapter a week ahead of your meeting time and do the individual activations at home. Then when you come together you can discuss how this went and encourage each other, using the questions provided in the study guide section to promote further discussion.

I know you will benefit greatly from the information and revelation you receive through this study. Your personal and collective creativity will be enhanced and your community will be blessed as you release the creativity and gifts that God has given each of you.

Please feel free to contact me if you have questions or want to share testimonies of the great things God has done in your life as a result of your creativity being released in new and exciting ways. Contact information is on the author page at back of this book.

HOW TO USE THIS BOOK

 *Creativity Activator*

- Buy yourself a journal and some colored pencils and pens of varying colored inks to use for the activations contained in this book. I suggest that your journal have blank unlined pages; that way you can write or draw wherever you like on the pages, unrestricted by lines.

- Consider creating a title page for your journal or decorating some of the pages of the journal, getting them ready for use. Go ahead and do that now. Decorate it as fancy or as plain as you want – draw borders, paint background washes on some pages, stick in some pictures that you can journal over and around, or leave it all plain and untouched, ready for whatever moves you when you begin each activation.

- Gather other supplies that you may need, like old magazines and newspapers to rip pictures and cut text from, a pair of scissors, glue, etc.

- You can check out some websites or Google "journaling" or "art journaling" online and you'll see plenty of examples that will give you inspiration. Bookshops like Amazon and Barnes and Noble will also have books on both journaling and art journaling that you can buy to inspire you.

Chapter One

What's so Important About Creativity?

Creativity is an intrinsic and essential part of being human. Without it we could not advance in any area of life.

Creativity is an amazing thing! Without it, nothing that exists would, in fact, exist. Creativity is both the source and the foundation on which personal life and society are built. Every advancement mankind has ever made has creativity at its source; indeed, it's the reason why civilization as we know it exists today. It's the seedbed and key to all ideas, invention, advancement in civilization, and problem solving. Nothing that man has created, and no problem that has been overcome, was done without creativity; it's that essential in every area of life.

Creativity is the process of an idea and its development. It connects inspiration, ideas, and thoughts together, and then develops them from conception to completion. Creativity sees possibilities, dreams, plans, and then takes what may seem to some to be little, seeming randomness – or even chaos (as in the case of God creating the universes) – and makes something of worth and value from those things.

Often when we think of creativity we think of great works of art or craft, books, music, movies and other such things, yet creativity is not restricted to the arts and crafts; it's far wider than that. The word "creativity" is often clouded with a sense of mystery and unobtainable genius, and it can seem like it's something that has been given to a few select people, but nothing could be further from the truth! Every single person that exists has the ability to be creative, and is able to apply that creativity to every area of their lives if they want to.

From artists to entrepreneurs, inventors to computer programmers, homemakers to chefs, office workers to athletes, we all use creativity daily. An idea comes and we follow it through, bringing something into being, whether in art or lifestyle. All of life, every part, is the result of creativity at work.

Naturally creative

Kids are naturally creative; they have an inbuilt sense of creativity, imagination, and curiosity. The whole world is their playground and they set off to explore it with abandonment. Their sense of creativity is unmatched and they take every possible opportunity to put it into practice – singing, dancing, coloring, making up stories, turning cardboard boxes into racing cars or forts, and using sticks for swords.

Yet as we grow, that natural creativity is trained out of us. We are naturally creative, individual, and independent thinkers, but we're trained to "fit in" instead – so we're taught to sit at desks, follow the rules, color inside the lines and stop our flights of imagination in order to concentrate on the subject at hand. How sad that is, and what a loss it's been to our world. The fact that we have to be trained to fit in tells us that we were created to be creative. We were created to stand out, to challenge the status quo and to bring change to the world we live in. Sadly, all too often, those who have kept and developed their creativity are now often viewed as rebels, misfits, and maybe even slightly odd. Yet the reality is that society has lost something incredibly special by trying to stifle and channel creativity for its own end, and ultimately we all suffer for it.

Let's look briefly at how a couple of dictionaries[1] define the word "create" and its related words "creative" and "creativity" –

- **Create** – Bring (something) into existence

- **Creative** – Relating to or involving the use of the imagination or original ideas to create something; The ability to produce original and unusual ideas, or to make something new or imaginative.

- **Creativity** – The state or quality of being creative. The use of imagination or original ideas to create something; inventiveness; the ability to transcend traditional ideas, rules, patterns, relationships, or the like, to create meaningful new ideas, forms, methods, interpretations, etc., originality, progressiveness or imagination.

Curiosity and creativity

Curiosity is a big part of sparking and growing creativity. Allow yourself to be curious because it is one of the foundations of creativity. Keep curiosity alive in your life. Curious people are

---
[1] Dictionaries used – Dictionary.com, Cambridge Dictionary, Merriam-Webster Dictionary, Oxford Dictionary

the discoverers; the pioneers of new frontiers in our world. Curiosity leads to discovery, discovery leads to creativity, and creativity leads to invention. Ask yourself what makes things work, why things are the way they are – could they be improved on, and how?

A man or woman without curiosity is someone whose life has ceased to be alive with hope. It's the life of someone who is just going through the motions, waiting until the time they die, or until someone rescues them from their prison of sameness.

Growing up, I thought Walt Disney was one of the most amazing persons alive. My childhood was filled with watching Mickey Mouse on TV and reading Donald Duck comics. I dreamed of being able to go to Disneyland and see this amazing place that imagination built. I longed to be like Walt, to bring happiness to people and make dreams live. Now as an adult I realize that Walt was a man who was curious about life and who surrounded himself with people like himself – creative people who were curious and dared to dream and explore possibilities.

Your curiosity and your creativity are among your most important attributes; feed them often, dare to dream, dare to take risks and to live outside of society's prescribed boxes. The future belongs to you. Let your creativity shape your life until it is one that makes you feel alive – joyously, supremely, audaciously alive!

Everyday creativity

Every day you are creative in hundreds of ways that feel so normal that you don't recognize the creativity in them. Researchers have recognized this and termed it "everyday creativity." Everyday creativity is creativity that we take for granted, the stuff we don't even really think about as being creative.

The mother who thinks up new ways to keep her children occupied, the entrepreneur who sees a need and fills it in the marketplace, teachers, shop assistants, chefs, office workers, engineers – they all use creativity every day in their jobs, home life, and undoubtedly in their relaxation as well, although they may not recognize it at the time.

Making our home a place where we feel comfortable and relaxed, as well as a place that expresses our personality, is creativity – imagined, thought through, planned and applied. Whenever we're creative we improve not only the world around us but our inner life, too. Our souls are fed by our creativity and our perceptions of beauty. It may be something that we've created or something created by someone else, but if we consider it pleasing, then a part of us gets fed by that.

Creativity – the key to problem solving

Every day of our life, multiple times a day, we use creativity. We often just don't recognize that we do so because its use is so instinctive. One of the big ways we use it is in problem solving. Problem solving is actually everyday creativity applied to whatever we are facing. In fact, no problem is ever solved without a creative process happening.

Creativity begins the moment we look at a problem in order to find a solution to it. Most of us instinctively take the first answer that presents itself, for expediency's sake, yet that first answer may not be the best answer. Try to look at your problems from different angles to come up with different solutions and, if possible, give yourself some time to do so. A lot of our problems aren't as urgent as we initially think, and we would find better answers to them if we allowed ourselves time to think about them.

The ultimate act of creativity – creating your life

Your life and what you make of it – that will be your most creative endeavor and possibly your greatest legacy. Every day you make decisions that form your life, and in doing so you create that life.

The problem comes when we abdicate the responsibility for creating our life and just let life happen to us. If we do so we will end up living a life that is a million miles away from the dream we once had. Yes, there will always be circumstances that happen that we didn't plan, or are beyond our control, but the truth is that we have a lot more control over how our life turns out than we sometimes want to acknowledge.

As children we naturally functioned in a high level of curiosity and creativity, but as we grew up, education and in many cases even family dynamics, told us to stop asking so many questions. As a result, for many people, curiosity –and subsequently, creativity – died a slow but definite death.

So we plod through life, living from day to day trying to earn enough in order to pay the bills, and the sameness of our daily life swallows up our creativity.

Take risks

Some people are afraid to be too curious. Why? Because curiosity may give rise to discontent, and discontent means having to think about the kind of life we're living. And if we think about it we may find that we hate it – we hate the sameness, the dullness of living day to day. Maybe we don't want to face that because it would mean that we have to do something about it, and that is too fraught with risk.

Usually it is fear of the unknown that keeps us from taking risks, yet it's precisely in facing fear that we make discovery – the discovery that there is more to us than we knew, more to life than we've dared to live. We discover that we have the creative power within us to change our world, to make something new of our life.

Dare to replace your fear of the unknown with curiosity again. Fear will bind you up, shut you down, cause you to turn inward and be trapped within yourself, but curiosity will take you into a lifetime of grand adventures. Our undertakings and experiences may not always be safe, they may not always be filled with ease, but they are always an adventure. And it's in that place of adventure that we discover new things.

As Christians, we realize that creating our life is actually a co-creating with God. He is ever present in the decisions we make, and Scripture tells us that Jesus came to give us *"life in all its fullness"* (John 10:10). It also tells us that we shouldn't just make our plans without involving Him in the decision-making process.

> Now listen you who say, "Today or tomorrow we will go to this or that city, spend a year there, carry on business and make money" ... Instead, you ought to say, "If it is the Lord's will, we will live and do this or that." —*James 4:13,15 NIV*

Don't let life set your course by default. Commit your way to the Lord, dream with Him about where your life could go and what you could achieve, and ask for His strategy for you to begin to co-create that life with Him (Psalm 48:14; 73:24; John 16:13).

Embrace your individuality

You are not like anyone else; you're a totally unique being. We understand that our fingerprints, voiceprints, and eye patterns are unique, but the things we like and the way we express ourselves are just as unique. Society tries daily in multiple ways to tell us that we have to conform, to fit in, to like the same things as others, yet we weren't created to live like that – squeezed into a mold of conformity. We were created to stand out in all our uniqueness and the innate beauty that is within that uniqueness. So do just that, express yourself, discover your likes and dislikes, and express your personality.

Be creative in how you dress, how you decorate your house, how you sign your name, how you present your meals – there are so many ways you can be creative in your everyday life. The following are a couple of simple examples of this in my life:

I used to hate the way I signed my name; my signature felt so immature and "schoolish." So one day I decided I would create a new signature. I sat down with paper and pen to create a whole lot of different signatures, until I found one I really felt at home with, and I adopted it. It took some practice to get used to, but I liked what my new signature said about me, so I persevered and got used to it, and I still use and love it today, over thirty years later.

Another time I decided that I was being too "safe" in how I dressed and presented myself. My childhood wounds told me that I shouldn't draw attention to myself or stand out, because people would notice me, and in my mind being noticed meant I would be picked on in all sorts of ways that would bring hurt and destruction into my life. When I finally realized that my wounds were holding me captive, I decided to do something about it. I got my hair dyed and started to wear clothes I actually liked. Now my hair is boldly colored with a streak that regularly changes color, and I wear clothes I love wearing that suit my personality, not my wounds.

Like me, you may have been hurt in life and decided to play it safe, but playing it safe doesn't do you or the world around you any good; it simply robs both of the creativity and expression that is uniquely you. Decide that you are going to do something about that. Get help if you need it, deal with the underlying wounds and issues that hold you down and repress who you really are, and let your creativity out again. We need you to be you; we need your uniqueness and creative expression in this world we live in.

Choose to live a creative life

Living a creative life doesn't just happen to us. We must choose to live one. We get to choose in large measure what our life will be like, how creative we want to be. Creativity is waiting within us for us to tap into it, but it will not force itself on us; we must choose it and choose to cooperate with it. How creative you are will largely be determined by how creative you want to be and how you view life. Recognizing the creativity that is within you is the first step, and then discovering what your creativity looks like and how to express it becomes a lifelong adventure.

Jeff Goins, blogger, writer, motivational trainer, says, "To release your creativity you must become more uncomfortable with standing still than with taking risks." He's right. Learn to get comfortable with taking risks. That doesn't mean you won't feel trepidation or uncertainty, it just means that it's okay to try something, to take a risk. You don't have to be perfect. It's okay to find out that you're not good at something, and it's okay to start with being bad at something and getting better at it as you go along.

Creativity Activator 1

Head up a new page titled: "I use creativity every day when…"

- Now, using loads of different colors, write down all the ways you can think of where you use creativity every day. Some examples:
    - ✓ I often take different routes to get to the same place;
    - ✓ thinking of new plays for the football team;
    - ✓ solving problems at work;
    - ✓ solving interpersonal relationship problems;
    - ✓ changing my home's décor;
    - ✓ thinking, "what if?"
    - ✓ finding distractions to keep my kids from fighting;
    - ✓ cooking…

- Take note as you go through today or tomorrow of all the different ways you used your creativity. Add them to this page. Becoming aware of how you use your creativity will cause greater thankfulness for it and greater use of it.

- It won't be long before your page is chock-full of the ways you employ creativity every day in your personal, work, and social life. When you think you've finished, sit back, relax, read over the list, and marvel at your creativity.

WHAT'S SO IMPORTANT ABOUT CREATIVITY?

 ## Creativity Activator 2

Take some time to think about your life. What do you want it to look like? What character traits do you want to develop? What good habits do you want to establish? What things would you like to accomplish? – Then do the following exercises, which will probably not be finished in one sitting, and you shouldn't place yourself under the pressure of having to do so. For me, they are lists that I have developed and added to over time, often coming back weeks or months later to add something new to them, or to cross off something I've accomplished on them.

- **Write a legacy or dreams list** – This list is about accomplishments and leaving a legacy. What are 20 things you want to accomplish in life that could leave a positive legacy? For example, write up your family history, write a book, start your own business, start a blog, start a kids club for underprivileged children, etc.

  Look at the list and see which one draws your attention. Why did this one draw your attention? Because it's easily achievable, or perhaps it's been your secret dream for forever? Ask yourself, what would stop you from doing this? What do you need to accomplish this – training, finances, etc.? What's the first step you could take towards accomplishing this dream?

- **Write a bucket list** – A "bucket" list is a list of things you'd like to experience. What are 20 things you want to experience before you die? Don't play safe in making the list. What you'd like to experience is what you'd like to experience; don't censor your list because you think something is too outrageous or too expensive. It could include such things as: bungee jumping, jet boating in Queenstown (New Zealand), having a facial, 10 pin bowling, learning to fly, or going overseas to ____. Look at the list and decide which one you want to do first. What's the first step you can take towards experiencing it?

Activating Declaration

Declare the following out loud over your life; don't hold back – do it with passion and volume. Speak it like you believe it – doing so will activate belief and agreement in your heart.

"I am alive. I am creative, and the future belongs to me. I have the power within me to change my world and pioneer something new in my life. My creativity is one of my most powerful attributes and I choose to embrace it wholeheartedly. I will live a creative, fulfilling life.

"I choose to embrace curiosity. Curiosity will lead me into discovery, and discovery will lead me into invention. I choose to shun fear that would lock me up; I choose to embrace the grand adventure that is life. I will revel in the adventure. I will boldly explore new territory and I'll live a life that is full and fulfilling.

"I choose to create for myself, and for those around me, a life that is full and rich, a life that recognizes my creativity and uses it to its fullest."

Chapter Two

God and Creativity

Creativity is, in its essence and at its source, life giving, because it comes from the very nature of God.

In the beginning, God created… The first picture of God we see in Scripture in Genesis is of God as the Creator, using His creativity.

In the beginning God created the heavens and the earth.
—Genesis 1:1

Even today we are still discovering some of the things that God created during that time, and no doubt we will continue to discover new things for a long time to come. God is the Creator and He is creative. Creativity is an intrinsic part of who He is; we cannot separate Him from His creativity. Without it He would be less than who He is.

Then Scripture tells us something amazing. It records a conversation that the Trinity had amongst themselves.

> Then God said, "Let us make man in our image, after our likeness. And let them have dominion over the fish of the sea and over the birds of the heavens and over the livestock and over all the earth and over every creeping thing that creeps on the earth." So God created man in his own image, in the image of God he created him; male and female he created them. And God blessed them. And God said to them, "Be fruitful and multiply and fill the earth and subdue it, and have dominion over the fish of the sea and over the birds of the heavens and over every living thing that moves on the earth."
> —*Genesis 1:26-28 ESV*

So mankind came into being as a result of the creative power and genius of God, as He sculpted a likeness out of clay and then breathed life into it, causing its substance to be changed from clay to living flesh. Wow!

Man is creative because God created man in His image. Creativity was built into mankind at creation and is an intrinsic part of being human. Right from the beginning, mankind's creativity was expressed in the naming of the animals and in the act of tending the ground. You may ask, "How is tending the ground creative? Isn't that just work?" When you understand creativity, what it is and what it does, then you realize that even in tending the ground, doing what may seem to some as a tedious job, people were using their creativity. They conceived, planned, worked their plan, and then the ground brought forth life. That's creativity at work right there.

What else does Scripture say about creativity – what its purpose is and how we use it? Scripture has a lot to say, and I'll share some in this chapter. For a more complete look at the subject you'll find a list of verses at the end of this book that you can study further.

GOD AND CREATIVITY

Early on in Scripture we see God acknowledging mankind's creativity when He refers to Lamech's family in Genesis:

> Lamech took to himself two wives: the name of the one was Adah, and the name of the other, Zillah. Adah gave birth to Jabal; he was the father of those who dwell in tents and have livestock. His brother's name was Jubal; he was the father of all those who play the lyre and pipe. As for Zillah, she also gave birth to Tubal-cain, the forger of all implements of bronze and iron... —*Genesis 4:19-22*

At this early point in our history, God simply acknowledges mankind's creativity. However, in Exodus we see God begin to put restrictions around it when He shares that creativity should not be used to make images of other gods or to worship those gods.

> "You shall have no other gods before me. You shall not make for yourself a carved image, or any likeness of anything that is in heaven above, or that is in the earth beneath, or that is in the water under the earth. You shall not bow down to them or serve them..." —*Exodus 20:3-5 ESV*

And again in Deuteronomy:

> "'Cursed be the man who makes a carved or cast metal image, an abomination to the LORD, a thing made by the hands of a craftsman, and sets it up in secret.' And all the people shall answer and say, 'Amen.'" —*Deuteronomy 27:15 ESV*

Other than that, God places no further restrictions around creativity and its use. He does, however, very much encourage people to use their creativity in relationship to their worshipping Him, as we see in Psalm 150 where He encourages the use of instruments, dance, and song. While these are the only expressions mentioned in this chapter, we need to realize that the tabernacle was a work of art in itself that featured works of great artistry in its decoration, the vessels used, the garments worn by the priest, the gold, embroidery, precious jewels, and timber that were used, and more.

In Exodus, chapters 25 to 28, we see the Lord begin to give to Moses the pattern for the tabernacle that would house His presence. We see that man's creativity was well developed by this point and that God encouraged the people to use it in their worship of Him. In these chapters is a wealth of knowledge that explains in detail the creativity and workmanship used, from dying fabrics to weaving and embroidery, woodwork to silver and goldsmithing, bronze and other metal work, engraving, sculpture, jewelry making, utensils and bowls. Later, in chapter 30, God instructs them in the mixing of fragrances for the oils for anointing the priests.

God clearly encourages and appreciates the use of creativity in our worship of Him, and doing so points us back to Him as the ultimate Creator, the one for whom creativity is as natural as breathing is to us.

Also in Exodus, we see that God not only made all people creative but that He anoints some people with creativity so that His name would be glorified and that people would be trained in creative endeavors.

> "See, the LORD has called by name Bezalel the son of Uri, the son of Hur, of the tribe of Judah. And He has filled him with the Spirit of God, in wisdom, in understanding and in knowledge and in all craftsmanship; to make designs for working in gold and in silver and in bronze, and in the cutting of stones for settings and in the carving of wood, so as to perform in every inventive work. He has also put in his heart

to teach, both he and Oholiab, the son of Ahisamach, of the tribe of Dan. He has filled them with skill to perform every work of an engraver and of a designer and of an embroiderer, in blue and in purple and in scarlet material, and in fine linen, and of a weaver, as performers of every work and makers of designs." —*Exodus 35:30-35*

In Exodus 36:1-2 we see that every skillful person whose heart was stirred to do so was called upon to work on the tabernacle, and they responded willingly.

This is important, as it gives us a baseline to work from as Christians. God gives our creative abilities to us and we are encouraged by Him to use them to bring glory to His name and to use them in His service, whatever those creative gifts and abilities are.

We see this reinforced in other Scriptures as well—

For we are his workmanship, created in Christ Jesus unto good works, which God hath before ordained that we should walk in them. —*Ephesians 2:10 KJV*

This verse tells us clearly that not only are we God's workmanship, but He has prepared good works for us to do. You are the workmanship of God and He has prepared for you "good works," works that will bring Him glory and give you a sense of fulfillment as you walk in His plans and use your creativity.

Whatever you do, work heartily, as for the Lord and not for men… —*Colossians 3:23 ESV*

Your life and your creativity have purpose, giving expression to the creativity God has placed in you, and in doing so, bringing Him glory. Doesn't that make you want to go and give expression to your creativity right now? It certainly makes me want to!

Throughout Scripture we see creativity used in many other ways, too. Here are some of them:

- In 1 Chronicles 22:15 we see stonecutters, masons, carpenters, and people skilled in working gold, silver, bronze, and iron.

- In 1 Chronicles 15 and 16 we see singers and musicians appointed to worship God.

- In Psalm 149:1 we are encouraged to sing spontaneous songs to the Lord.

- In Psalm 150:1-6 we are encouraged to use cymbals, tambourines, trumpets and other instruments to praise the Lord.

- In Psalm 150 we are also encouraged to use dance to praise the Lord.

- In Proverbs 31:20-24 we see a woman using her creativity to make clothing and household items of value and beauty to bring finances into her household.

- In 2 Timothy 3:16 and many other verses we see the use of the gift of writing (1 Kings 4:29-31; Psalm 45:1; Matthew 13:52).

- In Jeremiah 18:3 we see the creative work of the potter acknowledged.

- In Hosea 12:10 we see the use of prophetic mime and action. The prophets often used drama and mime to share their messages.

- In Mark 6:3 we see that Jesus was a carpenter.

- In Romans 12:6 we are encouraged to use our gifts.

- In the books of Matthew, Mark, Luke and John, we see Jesus using stories or parables many times to get a message across.

The above verses are just a few that refer to both God's creativity and ours. Mime is used over 40 times in Scripture. Over one-third of the ministry of Ezekiel is done in Jewish mime. Parables, as a form of storytelling, are used over 49 times, with a majority of these shared by Jesus. Parable, in a general sense, is seen over 250 times throughout the Old and New Testaments. The whole life of Hosea was a living prophetic drama. If we can understand the dramas and arts that took place in Scripture in a living, dramatic way, we will gain a richer comprehension of God's Word, and therefore, of God.

Scripture is full of references concerning creativity and its use, both in everyday life and in worship and service of God. God values creativity highly, and He openly encourages us to use it.

We know that God delights over us and even His delight is expressed creatively. In Zephaniah we read this:

"The LORD your God is in your midst, a victorious warrior.
He will exult over you with joy, He will be quiet in His love,
He will rejoice over you with shouts of joy."
—*Zephaniah 3:17*

God doesn't just tell us that He delights in us, but He expresses that delight creatively with His whole being. Not only does God sing over you, but the term "exult over you with joy" can also be translated "to whirl or spin around (with joy or gladness)." In other words, God Himself dances with delight over you! You have been made in the image of the God of all creativity – the singing, dancing, rejoicing God!

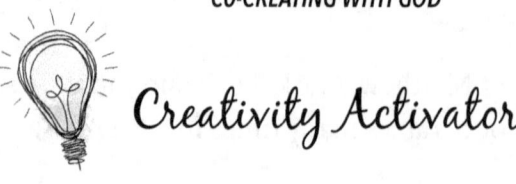

Creativity Activator

In this activation you will be forming an affirmation or declaration to speak over your life.

- Take a couple of the verses shown either in this chapter or at the end of the book, and personalize them by forming them into a declaration you can make over your own life, as in the example below.

- Write them out in your journal (be creative in how you do so, using color, different styles of writing, etc.) Also explain how they make you feel as you read them. Do you believe them, or is something within you resisting their goodness working in your life? If so, explore that. Ask why and where that resistance stems from. Talk to God about it and ask Him to help you with that.

- Write your affirmation on a Post-it note or a piece of paper, and put it where you can see it frequently. Or you may even choose to use window marker pens and write the affirmation on your mirror where you'll see it as you get dressed each morning.

- Decree that affirmation over your life on a regular, preferably daily, basis for the next couple of months. In doing so you are helping to form and establish in the brain new neural pathways of belief, which you will then be able to live in the light of.

Sample Affirmation

Genesis 1:26 and 31 say that God made mankind in His image and then He declared that what He'd made was very good. That could become a declaration similar to the following:

"I'm made in the image of God who is the ultimate Creator. He has given me creativity as a confirmation that I'm made in His image. Therefore I am created to create! My creativity is very good, it's a blessing to me and it will be a blessing to others. I am a creative being, and I was born to live a creative life. I'll do so with joy and I'll relish the adventure of discovering new areas of creativity within me."

You could use the above declaration, but I encourage you to ask God to highlight verses to you so that you can create your own declarations. That way you are using your creativity and allowing the Lord access to your beliefs about it.

Chapter Three

Imagine That!

Imagination's purpose is not to escape life, but to create it! Everything that was ever created started in someone's imagination.

Imagination is not our enemy. It is not evil, and using it is not "wasting time," as you'll discover in this chapter. Yet many of us have been taught, either directly or indirectly, that it is. We may have come to believe that our imagination is primarily just a place where we fantasize or dream up errant behavior. Or maybe it has become an escape from reality, as it was for me for some of my life.

Because of what we've been taught, many of us place a very low value on the use of our imagination and, consequently, on creativity. Sometimes we can recognize that imagination has a place in our life, yet still limit it to certain areas, thinking that it only applies to art, writing, or other such "creative" pursuits.

Suppressing your imagination is actually a dangerous practice that can lead to all sorts of problems in life. Why? Because when you suppress it, you suppress an intrinsic part of who you are and how you were made.

Let's look at where our imagination came from and what our imagination is for. The Bible says that God created mankind in His image, and with that He gave to us the faculty of creativity and imagination. Creativity is not just something God does; it's who He is – so much so that He's named "the Creator."

Imagination in Scripture

In the Bible we see God's creative imagination or thoughts manifested physically in the creation of the universe, earth, and mankind. Man, being made in His image, received the ability to imagine, conceive vision, and see it brought to manifested fruition. Adam and Eve had an imagination, and God called on Adam to use that imagination and creativity right from the outset when He asked Adam to name the animals.

The Hebrew nation recognized that God had given man creativity and imagination, and they referred to it often in their Scriptures in reference to both the good and bad use of it.

Before the "fall" of mankind in the Garden of Eden, man's mind and imagination operated in purity and wholeness. But when the "fall" happened, Scripture tells us that man's heart, mind, and imagination became darkened and were given over to base desires.

> For even though they knew God, they did not honor Him as God or give thanks, but they became futile in their speculations, and their foolish heart was darkened. —*Romans 1:21*

In the Hebrew understanding, the heart, mind, and imagination are linked, and they all play a part in our imagination.

In Ephesians, the phrase "eyes of the heart" and "eyes of the mind," or "eyes of the understanding" is used, depending on what version of Scripture you read. While those phrases sound poetic, they actually have a very real meaning and refer to how we see internally. The meaning of all three phrases is the same and refers to the use of our imagination.

In Ephesians, Paul prays –

> That the God of our Lord Jesus Christ, the Father of glory, may give unto you the spirit of wisdom and revelation in the knowledge of him: the eyes of your understanding being enlightened; that ye may know what is the hope of his calling... —*Ephesians 1:17-18 KJV*

The word "understanding" in that verse is the word *dianoia*, which means deep thought, imagination, mind and understanding. So Paul is praying that our imagination and understanding, which work together, would be opened so we may know the hope of our calling... Somehow, our imaginations, our ability to see and conceive things and receive revelation are all a vital part of understanding.

Then in Colossians we see something wonderful; it tells us that when we were saved, our imagination was sanctified and set apart for God.

> And you, who once were alienated and enemies in your mind by wicked works, yet now He has reconciled [made right with him]... —*Colossians 1:21 NKJV*

(In this verse the word translated as *mind* actually means "imagination" in the original Greek.)

So we now have sanctified imaginations and we no longer have to walk in the futility of our darkened mind alone.

We now get to walk in a whole new way.

> So this I say, and affirm together with the Lord, that you walk no longer just as the Gentiles also walk, in the futility of their mind [logical reasoning mind], being darkened in their understanding [imagination], excluded from the life of God… But you did not learn Christ in this way… Put on the new self, which in the likeness of God has been created in righteousness and holiness of the truth."
> —*Ephesians 4:17-18, 20, 24*

How do we put on the new self in regard to our imagination? By knowing what God says about it, by seeing ourselves living like that in our imagination, by being renewed in our minds, and by acting in line with what that new creation self looks like.

> Do not be conformed to this world, but be transformed by the renewing of your mind, so that you may prove what the will of God is, that which is good and acceptable and perfect. —*Romans 12:2*

> Neglect not the gift that is in thee, which was given thee by prophecy, with the laying on of hands... Meditate upon these things; give thyself wholly to them; that thy profiting may appear to all. —*1 Timothy 4:14-15 KJV*

The word "meditate" in this verse is the Greek word *meletao* which means "to revolve in the mind, to imagine." In other words, imagine yourself doing what God has called you to do; see yourself doing what was prophesied over you. Give yourself wholly to this, and then you will prosper.

Moses understood how to use his imagination. *"By faith he forsook Egypt, not fearing the wrath of the king; for he endured, as seeing him who is invisible*" (Hebrews 11:27 KJV). The word *seeing* means "to stare at, to discern clearly either physically or mentally." Moses saw the Lord face to face, physically and mentally.

Scripture tells us we can even use our imagination in loving God.

> "...love the Lord your God with all your heart, and with all your soul, and with all your mind [imagination]."
> —*Matthew 22:37*

How would we do that? One way is by recalling to our mind and vision center the times God has been faithful to us and the revelations He has shown us, as well as the experiences we've had of Him. Recalling these things causes thankfulness and love to well up in our hearts.

Imagination's purpose

So why was our imagination given to us and what is it used for? It's your dream/vision center, it's where you conceive dreams and ideas that you can then begin to bring into reality – songs, art, new inventions, etc. Your imagination is a creative place within your mind. It involves the use of several centers of your brain that work together to access imagination.

Could it be that God values imagination and wants it to be used in conjunction with logic and reasoning? Scripture would appear to imply that.

> Now unto him that is able to do exceedingly abundantly above all that we ask or think, according to the power that worketh in us."
> —*Ephesians 3:20 KJV*

In the New International Version, this verse says that God can do immeasurably, even more than what we imagine. Our reasoning mind will always try to talk us down, try to make us see sense, and try to tell us that we must be reasonable. But why must we, when God is able to do exceedingly abundantly above that, according to the power – His power – that works in us?

Imagination's other purpose

Your imagination is not just where you dream and plan, however; it has a spiritual job to do, too. You are a spiritual being. Your spirit is the very core or essence of your being, and your spirit, soul and body cooperate and work together.

Your imagination functions in conjunction with these three aspects – spirit, soul and body. Your internal vision center (imagination/mind) can receive and process information and revelation from the spirit realm as well as from the natural realm. It can operate like a frequency receiver (like a TV) that can be tuned to pick up the frequencies of the spiritual realms. When it does, they appear as internal visions that can be either clear, full color visions, or faint impressions. Neither is more real than the other; they are just seen with differing amounts of clarity. Receiving visual revelation allows us to see the normally unseen realm of the Kingdom of Heaven. Scripture tells us that we should fix our eyes on seeing the unseen things.

> "…we look not at the things which are seen [visible], but at the things which are not seen [not visible in this realm]; for the things which are seen are temporal, but the things which are not seen are eternal." *—2 Corinthians 4:18*

How do we see the normally unseen things, the things that are invisible to the naked eye? Through the eyes of faith! Faith activates internal sight and it gives us insight and understanding far beyond the ability of the reasoning mind alone.

Revelation is received from the spiritual realms by your spirit, then transmitted to your natural mind, where it can be received either as thoughts or pictures. Your reasoning mind then kicks into gear and begins to try to understand and make sense of the information it has received.

We all receive information from the spiritual realms, we often just don't know that we are; we think that all our thoughts originate with us. It's what we do with the information that we receive that determines whether good or evil is hatched and manifested.

Imagination's role in behavior

We've probably all heard preachers say this… "As a man thinks in his heart, so he is." Your imagination can, and does, have a direct effect on your behavior. Your imagination is the birthplace of all your behavior and has a huge effect on the reality you walk in. All your actions start first in your thought life. If you accept that thought picture and dwell on it, then your reasoning mind begins to work with your imagination and plans how you can achieve that thing.

So you see, you and your imagination have an important part to play! Your imagination is the seedbed for so much, and out of your imagination will come business ideas, works to help humanity, artworks, and so much more. You get to dream them and bring them to fruition with God's help – you get to co-create with God!

"For as he thinks in his heart, so is he." —*Proverbs 23:7 NKJV*

Above all else guard your heart, for everything you do flows from it. —*Proverbs 4:23 NIV*

Casting down imaginations, and every high thing that exalteth itself against the knowledge of God, and bringing

into captivity every thought to the obedience of Christ.
—*2 Corinthians 10:5 KJV*

Keep your imagination and the thoughts of your heart in check; bring them into a place of submission to Christ so that you may live the kind of life that He has for you – one that is good, pure, and full of wholesome creativity.

If you've been using your imagination in a wrong way, for example in viewing pornography, then ask the Lord to help you bring it under control and to cleanse it. Break the power of addiction over your life; many of these things have an addictive quality to them. Seek help if need be, so you can rebuild your thought life in a healthy way; there are pastors, counselors and groups that can help you.

Imagination and fear

We know that imagination has a big part to play in the work of fear in our life, too. Scripture tells us in several places that we should not let fear get an upper hand in our lives. Part of controlling fear is controlling our imagination or thought life.

"Do not seek what you should eat or what you should drink, nor have an anxious mind [imagination]."
—*Luke 12:29 NKJV*

Whatever is true, whatever is honorable, whatever is right, whatever is pure, whatever is lovely, whatever is of good repute, if there is any excellence and if anything worthy of praise, dwell on these things. —*Philippians 4:8*

Many times we are told in Scripture to "fear not." Because the Lord is with us, we need not fear, whatever may come our way. Scripture also tells us in Isaiah 26:3 that our minds can know perfect peace when they are fixed on Him.

You will guard him and keep him in perfect and constant peace whose mind [both it's inclination and its character] is stayed on You. —*Isaiah 26:3 AMPC*

Fear has a huge impact on creativity; it can shut it down and keep us from stepping out, trying new things, and knowing a fulfilling creative life, if we let it. But remember this – fear is mostly "smoke and mirrors," it's the voice of intimidation speaking to you to stop you from stepping into freedom to be who you were created to be. On the other side of fear is breakthrough, enlargement, and pleasure. Push past fear; don't let it build false boundaries around your life.

Fear has a voice. Realize that, in many cases, when fear speaks it is an external voice talking to your heart from the spirit realm. It is not based on fact and certainty, but on possibility; don't listen to it! When fear speaks, you have authority over it and you can ask the Lord His opinion on what fear is saying.

It's just your imagination

Our children are born believing that anything is possible. It's us adults who tend to squash that by saying things like, "It's just your imagination" or "Stop daydreaming, go and do something productive." Or maybe we look at their creative attempts and try to "fix them up," thereby telling our children that their creativity isn't good enough. Many people's imaginations and creativity are shut down to some degree because as children they somehow got the message that their imagination wasn't of any value and that it would just get in their way in the real world.

Many of you will find these words resonating within you because you've had your imagination or creativity squashed as a child, or maybe you've squashed someone else's inadvertently by things you've said. Maybe someone inadvertently or deliberately squashed your imagination or creativity as a child and you then began to partner with that, inhibiting and thwarting it as you continued to grow.

However, all is not lost. It's not too late to remove the binding power that those words or acts have had over you. They may have held you locked up, but today you can get free from their hold and move forward in a new release of creativity that will continue to grow as you feed and nurture it. How do you do that? To a degree, it's already started. Truth is entering you and is beginning to go to work – the truth that your imagination, your creativity, is good, and that it's a gift from God that releases new and wonderful things into your life and, through you, into others' lives. Also, at the end of this chapter you'll find a declaration and prayer for the effects of that squashing to be broken over your life.

> "Whatever you ask for in prayer, believe that you have received it, and it will be yours." —*Mark 11:24 NIV*

That means that your prayer will set things in motion in the spirit realm and bring the freedom from that realm into this one for you. You can then activate that reality by stepping out and beginning to create. Whether that creativity manifests in your workplace as creative ideas, at an art table, or in a garage workshop doesn't matter. You are releasing your creativity to get to work and bring changes and new realities into your world.

Also, don't automatically dismiss your daydreams; they're an important part of the creative process – they are your imagination at work! In fact, it's important to give yourself time to daydream. You never know what may come as a result of doing so – maybe an invention that will change the world, or maybe an artwork that will deeply touch people's hearts. Set aside a few minutes each day to just daydream; set your imagination to work and see what good things come as a result. Journal what you daydream and then you'll see which ideas are worth dreaming about some more, or putting into action.

As you can see, our imagination is far more complex and powerful than we've given it credit for but, oh, what fun discovering its abilities!

Now do the creative activators below; pray or declare the truth about your creativity and imagination (using the activating prayer) and see yourself set free from the limiting beliefs and negative binding words spoken over you.

Creativity Activator 1

Use the following prayer or your own words to declare your freedom from the limits that have held your imagination back from functioning as it should, and to express your intent to be free in valuing and using your imagination.

"God, thank You for my vision center, my imagination, which Scripture says is the eyes of my understanding. I come into agreement with You regarding it; my imagination is good and glorious! I'm sorry for where I've allowed my imagination to be filled with rubbish and things that are not good or helpful to me. Cleanse and renew my imagination so that I may use it in the way that You intended it to be used – to receive revelation, to see and to create.

"I come out of agreement with the binding power of any negative words that have been spoken over me, by myself or by others, concerning my imagination and creativity. I come into agreement with truth – that my imagination has great importance and my creativity is valuable! I refuse to listen to the voice of fear and intimidation. Instead, I choose to listen to You and to fix my mind on You, knowing that You will give me peace.

"Open my eyes to see the possibilities in the situations I find myself in daily. You have already given me permission to be creative by making me in Your image, so I choose to allow myself to think creatively. I give myself permission to think outside the box and to allow my creativity to blossom. Thank you, God, for renewed and released creativity in my life. Amen."

 *Creativity Activator 2*

- Look at how you've viewed and used your imagination in the past. Does it line up with Scripture and how God sees your imagination? Journal about that. Ask God to help you recover and retrain your imagination to function properly again.

- Set aside some time to dream, to imagine. Begin with something simple – the aim is to help you retrain yourself in seeing internally.

- Remember a time when you had great fun as a kid, or even more recently. Let the memory fill your mind and allow yourself to feel the pleasure of it again.

- Or imagine your bedroom as you left it this morning. See where everything is, where the clothes are, what color the curtains are, etc. Recall as much detail as you can.

- Or dream about an area in your life and how you could improve it. Imagine what it would be like once those improvements were established. Let yourself construct mental images of that; see it. Now, ask what's needed for that dream to come to pass, and set about to bring it to pass.

- Your natural mind will try to tell you that it's a waste of time, but it's not; it's actually very important time. At first you might find your mind wandering off to work topics or arguing with you that you're being lazy or wasting time. Tell it to be quiet, and that you'll get back to other work soon but, for now, this is the work you should be doing. Refocus and allow yourself to imagine again.

Chapter Four

Losing Me, Finding Me
Creativity and the Loss of It

*The greatest loss is that which dies inside
while you are still alive.*

As children, we didn't need to be taught to be creative, we just were; it was instinctive – boxes became castles or racing cars, sticks became swords, chalk and crayons were magical things that let us use color in ways no sophisticated adult would dream of. We colored outside the lines, used bold slashes of color, and held our work up to show Mum or Dad, so proud of what we had done.

Slowly, however, we became aware that it's considered better to color within the lines, to restrict our color palette, and to keep our imaginations inside our head. By the time we were teens we classified "unrestricted creativity" as being babyish, and we sought instead to take our cues from those around us so that we would be accepted. The teen years are often filled with uncertainty as we try so hard to "fit in," and peer pressure plays a huge part in many people shutting down their creativity for fear of being labeled.

We are all born with highly functioning creativity, and studies have shown that at the age of five, 90% of children operate in a high level of it. But unfortunately for most of us, somewhere along the way we either lose, or get talked out of, our creativity until as adults the use of highly functioning creativity is down to approximately 2% of people.

Pablo Picasso said, "Every child is an artist. The problem is how to remain an artist once he grows up." For some people that loss seems to be not a big deal, but for others – they spend most of their adult years wishing or hoping that they could somehow get that freedom and creativity back again.

Adobe, in their "State of Create" benchmark study done in 2012,[2] came up with some surprising conclusions regarding creativity in adult lives. In the research, they interviewed 5,000 adults from a range of countries. Less than half of those interviewed described themselves as creative, and only a quarter felt that they were living up to their creative potential. Over half of those interviewed believe that the education system stifles creativity rather than encourages it. These statistics show us very clearly that we believe creativity is foundational and necessary in our daily lives, yet it also shows that we don't know how to nurture and develop it as we go through life.

For many of us, the loss of creativity has critical and often debilitating effects because it is the loss of an essential and very important part of who we were created to be.

Loss of Creativity

Loss of our creativity can be caused by many things – active discouragement from others, comparison to others, our own

---

[2] Adobe "State of Create" benchmark study http://www.adobe.com/aboutadobe/press-room/pdfs/Adobe_State_of_Create_Global_Benchmark_Study.pdf

negative self image, the pressure to perform well, having to put your energy into just surviving, or simply believing the lie that says, "I'd love to paint, to dance, to write – but I can't do it."

I come from a family of nine children. Most of us love to create in some form or another, from jewelry making to writing, woodworking, sculpting, knitting, fine-art painting, or other creative pursuits. And yet even amongst my siblings, there are some who look at the other siblings' talents and creativity, measure themselves against it, and come up wanting in their own eyes.

Every one of us has creativity within us, waiting to be stirred up and released, and it is never too late to do so. There's much more to us than we currently know, but if we don't take the chance we will never know what gift may lie hidden dormant within us. It's simply a matter of finding your creative expression, whether that is found in business, hospitality, the arts, or somewhere else!

Creativity Killers

There are many creativity killers, or things that would try to quash your creativity. Below are just a few…

- **The Comparison trap** – It is possible to acknowledge that you have some creativity, but still think of yourself as not being very creative. How do I know that? Because I've done exactly that at various times in my life. The main cause of that is very simple – I compared myself to others.

    Comparison is a creativity killer. Falling into the trap of comparing yourself with others will always have an effect on you. It stops you from recognizing and appreciating your uniqueness and from developing that uniqueness so that others are blessed by it.

When we compare ourselves with others, one of two things can happen. Either the comparison comes off favorably for us, or it doesn't. Both have their traps. If the comparison comes off favorably for us, we may become satisfied with our state and think we don't need to develop our creativity any more. If the comparison comes off unfavorably, we may be discouraged and even end up thinking it's not worth trying.

To deal with this creativity killer, recognize that you are unique, and understand your current abilities. We do need to be able to honestly assess our abilities, but that is different from comparing ourselves with others. Assessing our abilities shows us what areas are strengths and what are currently weaknesses; it shows where we need to grow and areas that we may need to give more time or focus to. We also need to learn how to assess our work without our identity being threatened by that assessment. Your work is not who you are; it is simply something you have created, however dear to your heart that creation is. Don't get your works and your identity mixed up; nothing good lies down that path.

- **Fear** – Fear is a creativity killer. If you let it, fear will shut you down, lock you up and walk away gloating. Fear plays a huge part in people not releasing their creativity: the fear of not being good enough, not being accepted, being thought a failure or a fraud, finding out that you don't have what it takes. Then there's the fear of success, of being able to handle being seen, of exposure, and so much more that it's overwhelming ... and that's another one, the fear of being overwhelmed, aargh! An important thing to remember is that fear is about smoke screens and mirrors; it's about limitation and building false boundary lines around your life.

To deal with this creativity killer, recognize that the enemy of your soul wants to shut you down and build false boundary lines around your life. Realize that fear is simply a scary doorway, and on the other side of that doorway is freedom, breakthrough, and growth. Challenge the giants that stand at that door. Push past them and they will give way because that is their nature also – they are fearful, of *you*. That's why they intimidate with bluster and bravado – they are afraid of you!

- **Pressure to perform** – Pressure to have to come up with something – to *have* to be creative – can be a creativity killer, especially if deadlines are involved. When we are under pressure, the fight, flight or freeze syndrome kicks in. If our response is to fight, it can lead to physical and psychological symptoms that shut down the brain, causing us to be unable to think clearly. The flight and freeze reactions can cause an inability to face the pressure and shut us down or cause us to "run away" by procrastinating or abdicating our responsibility.

  To deal with this creativity killer, learn to identify your typical responses to pressure. Stand up to it. You have the power to be in control of both your feelings and your external circumstances. Find ways to balance your time, make lists, formulate a plan that works for you. Learn ways to cope with stress; read up on ways to do that, and put them into practice.

- **Unrealistic expectations** – Many of us place unrealistic expectations around our creativity, and others do, too. We want to do it well, to get it right, even make it perfect. Other people may have unrealistic expectations based on what they need, not necessarily on our ability, but there are times when people think we can do stuff that we can't, and they ask more of us than we are able to deliver.

To deal with this creativity killer, learn how to deal with unrealistic expectations – yours and others. Realize you don't have to be perfect, whatever "perfection" is in your mind. You are on a growth journey; enjoy the journey. Don't be afraid to say something if you feel that what is being asked is beyond your capability. Negotiate; ask if those requirements are set in concrete, and look for, then offer, other alternatives.

- **Meeting the needs and demands of others** – This could be either family or work demands on your time, or it could be creating what others say you should create, rather than what you enjoy. It could be having to create in a restrictive atmosphere of duty and obligation, which brings resentment.

  To deal with this creativity killer – Think about the times when you're most happy creating. What sort of thing brings you pleasure and feelings of value? Look at your creative life honestly and evaluate some things. Do you like the type of thing you're creating? What sort of work are you producing? Are you doing a particular kind of creative work simply because it's needed? Do you get to try new things that stimulate you? What have you always wanted to try creatively? Look at ways you can incorporate more of these things into your creative life.

- **Routine** – Too much routine, or not enough routine – either of these extremes can be creativity killers.

  To deal with this creativity killer – If it is too much routine, make sure you allow yourself time to be curious, to explore, to learn and to seek out new things outside your usual routine. If it is too little routine – work on any tendency to let yourself get sidetracked by every new exciting thing that comes up in a day. Fight apathy and laziness. Schedule in time to be creative, go places, and explore new possibilities.

Recovering your Creativity

While there may have been things that stole or quashed your creativity in earlier life, it's not too late to recover it and rediscover the wonder of using it, of finding yourself again. Are you ready to recover and rediscover your creativity?

Determine today to do so; it's a decision that you won't regret. The creativity activator at the end of this chapter will help get you started on the process of recovery, but you can also do other things that will help, too.

- Seek help and counsel if you need to deal with unresolved issues regarding your creativity.

- You recover and discover your creativity by being pro-active. Think about the areas of creativity that interest you, then actively seek ways you can get involved in those particular areas, so you can recover and express your creativity. Go to some workshops, take lessons, or seek out groups of people who are interested in the same things as you, and join them.

- Practice your creativity regularly – look for ways you can use it every day, make space and time in your life and home to express yourself creatively. Consider setting aside an area of your home for creative pursuits – a cupboard for keeping supplies in, a desk to work at, and a pinboard for pinning ideas on. It doesn't have to be "flashy," and don't over-decorate it; it needs to be a useable space. If you decorate it too much, you won't want to mess the area up and instead will put off creating there.

Creativity Activator

Open your journal to a fresh page and head it up with "Where am I at?" This activation is an evaluation of where you are at in regards to your creativity. Look at your creative expression honestly and ask yourself some questions, writing the answers in your journal. Some of the things you could ask are…

- In what ways was my creativity squashed as a child or as an adult, and what can I do about that?
- What do I feel about my creativity at this point in time?
- Am I expressing it in the way I want to?
- What creativity killers do I recognize at work in my life?
- How am I going to combat them?

Now, take some time to talk to the Lord about your journaling. Ask Him to heal any soul wounds that have come from your creativity having been shut down. Forgive those who need forgiving. Get someone to pray with you if you need to.

- Ask the Lord what He feels about your creativity, and write that across the bottom of the page in big, bold, colorful letters. This is the truth from God that sets you free and trumps all other beliefs.
- You could also do some art therapy in relation to this. Basically, art therapy uses drawing and color to release the emotion and feelings relating to events that have happened. Draw or paint a picture relating to your creativity and how you feel about it, using color mark making (let the color and density of the marks you make express your emotion).

Another option is to cut out pictures and words and paste them into the drawing. Process as you do this; let yourself recognize and feel the emotions, whether pleasure or sadness. Forgive anyone who needs to be forgiven, and let any hurt go. To find out more on art therapy, check out the books and websites listed below in the footnote.[3]

---

[3] The Art Therapy Sourcebook – Cathy A. Malchiodi, http://intuitivecreativity.typepad.com/expressiveartinspirations/100-art-therapy-exercises.html

Chapter Five

Oh, the Possibilities!
Discovering Your Creativity Potential

How do you find what you're good at?
You let curiosity loose.
A creative life is a curiosity rich life.

Everyone is creative, and there are no exceptions to that! You may find your creativity is best expressed in the business world as an entrepreneur, or it may be that you find a creative outlet in invention, architecture or building, cooking, home design, music, singing, dance, writing, painting, knitting, or woodwork. The possibilities are endless, and there will be at least one that is the right fit for you. There are areas of creativity that will suit you, your personality and your skills; sometimes it is just a matter of trying things until you discover which ones suit you. Give yourself permission to experiment and discover, to find out whether you enjoy something or not. You'll never know until you give it a go.

Some people will find their greatest joy in one particular way of expressing their creativity while others will try and succeed in many different arenas and expressions. Don't limit yourself by thinking that now you've found something you can do, that this is it, that "this will be my creative outlet for the rest of my life." Thinking like that will limit you; most people can usually become good at multiple expressions. Most often, it is simply a matter of taking the time to learn how to do them, and you will probably find that one thing appeals to you more than others. It's usually best to concentrate on developing one area of creativity at a time; otherwise, if your focus is spread too widely, you can end up doing a mediocre job in learning any of them.

I remember many years ago seeing my brother-in-law attend art classes, and I was wishing I could paint. I lost count of the times I said to him, "I wish I could paint, but I can't even draw." After about a year of me saying that, one day he told me that I was coming to the next class with him. I was sure I would be shown up as an art failure, but the teacher was patient and had a great technique for teaching beginners. At the end of that day I came home with a painting that was obviously amateurish but was far better than I had expected I could ever do. Something was awakened within me, and I went to many of that teacher's art workshops after that, developing my skills until I felt I was good enough to show my work. I ended up holding solo exhibitions, sold my work in several galleries, and even won a couple of prizes in art shows that I entered. I still love painting to this day, but I would never have discovered it if I hadn't faced my fears and given it a go.

As I said earlier, creativity is the key to all advances in civilization, to invention, and to problem solving. We probably don't think that working in a shop or an office is creative, yet even in situations like these we must use creativity to solve the problems we face. Creativity is important in every area of your life – relationships, work, pastimes and hobbies, and even your spiritual life. As I have already stressed, creativity is not just for art and crafts, although I believe that having a creative pastime will enhance your life and creativity in every area. By giving ourselves permission to be creative at a hobby level, we will more likely transfer those creative skills to other areas.

Creativity is not restricted to one gender over the other, and no area of creativity is gender-defined, either; there are men who enjoy knitting and embroidery just as there are women who enjoy woodworking and welding. Don't pigeonhole yourself or put limits on your creativity.

There are many reasons for creating – one is simply for the pleasure of creating, to let what's inside of us out; or we may use that creativity to say something – to get our point of view across, or to touch and help others. One reason is not right and the others wrong – they are simply different parts of a whole. To create for the pleasure of creating is glorious fun, and when something you've created touches someone's heart, you realize that there is still more waiting for you.

There's more to you than you know

You'll never know what's hidden inside you or how good you'll be at something until you try it. "There's more to you than you think" – this saying has inspired many over the years and has been used time and time again in literature, movies and as inspiration for people's lives. Gandalf, as he talks to Bilbo in The Hobbit, Louisa May Alcott in Little Women, and many others, have taken this saying and used it in some form or another. I remember reading about a man named Kurt Hahn who saw that quote on a wall in Belgium. It inspired him so much that it became his life motto, as well as the motto for a school he founded. His life's calling was to help people around the world realize this truth about themselves.

The urge to create is resident within each one of us, and with this book I want you to realize that you can discover, or rediscover, and release that creativity.

Don't repress your creativity – it's dangerous!

Creativity should never be repressed – to do so can lead to all sorts of horrible reactions within us. Creativity is often an outlet for emotions, and if we don't express them on a regular basis we are likely to suppress them. Suppressing emotions is never good, and if we try to, they will come back to bite us another day. Suppressing your creativity can lead to irritability, anger, fatigue, and lack of motivation. Sicknesses of various kinds, lethargy, loss of enthusiasm for life, depression, inattention to details, loss of awareness and the like are not uncommon, as well as general feelings of sadness and loss. While many people may not be able to pinpoint the origins of that feeling of loss, I believe much of it comes because we have shut down an essential part of who we are – our creative selves.

So don't repress that creativity, let it out, express yourself! If you do so, you and those around you will see the benefits.

The Possibilities Are Endless

There are so many types of creativity to try. Below is a list of areas to explore, although it's not exhaustive by any means. You may try one and not like it; that's fine, try another. There will be a creative expression that suits you. And when you find it, not only will it bring you enjoyment but you'll find your whole life benefits from your creativity.

- Art – painting, drawing, mixed media work, fabric art, illustration
- Comedy – stand up comedy, script writing, joke books
- Cooking – creating recipes, cookbook creation, baking
- Craft – Sewing, knitting, crochet, floral design, china doll making
- Dance – cultural, social, choreography, worship dance
- Design – graphic design, architecture, interiors, clothing design, toy design, game and puzzle design
- Doodling – zentangle, sketch-noting, graffiti, coloring book design, mind-mapping[4]
- Fashion – design, creation, make-up artistry
- Glass blowing and molding
- Jewelry making – take classes, use fabrics, paper, recycled articles, fimo, try silver work or gold work, (check out my Pinterest Jewelry pages for ideas)[5]
- Journaling – written, art journaling, Bible journaling, spiritual life journal, prayer journal
- Mosaics
- Music – singing, playing an instrument, beat-boxing, busking, joining an a cappella group

---

[4] Mind-mapping – http://www.mind-mapping.co.uk/mind-mapping-information-and-advice/how-to-make-a-mind-map/
http://learningfundamentals.com.au/blog/dont-understand-something-break-it-down-with-mindmaps/
[5] https://nz.pinterest.com/lynpacker/

- Pottery – also Polymer clay work. Paper making and papier-mâché.

- Photography – nature, architecture, people; check out Instagram to see how people use photography every day

- Recycling – taking old things and repurposing them to make them useful again

- Sculpture – metal, wood, stone, recycled parts

- Sewing – clothing, patchwork, design and make cloth handbags, make dolls, reuse old clothes or fabric to create new things

- Teaching – hobby classes, exercise classes, school, adult education, languages, teach repurposing classes where old items are transformed into new things

- Technology – computer-based art, graphic design, computer programming, cell phone app design, video clips and small films, web broadcasts, Facebook live clips

- Theatre – acting, production, set design, costume design and creation

- Writing – articles, short stories, poetry, novels, non-fiction books, comic books, children's books, blogs (a regularly updated website written in informal or conversational style)

I recently read a great article on creating a reverse bucket list of your creative pursuits.[6] The purpose of the list was to remind yourself of how often you had used your creativity already in your lifetime. I especially liked the way the writer shared how we should

---

[6] http://www.createintandem.com/make-reverse-bucket-list-creative-pursuits/

approach it from a positive viewpoint, that of knowing that "we are more than what we do."

What you need in order to start creating

To start creating or making things, look around and see what you already have at hand. Sometimes we think we have to have all the right specialist tools in order to start creating, but that is not true. Creativity can easily happen without any of the creative tools we think we need. You can create amazing things from everyday objects and a little inventiveness. If you have a pen or pencil you can do amazing works of art. Just check out pen drawings on Google Images and you'll see what I mean. A food grater can become a kitchen lamp with a little creativity and a light fitting. A stack of suitcases can become a storage solution as well as a décor statement. Those branches that were left over after pruning the olive tree can become a stylish door wreath. A pocketknife and a piece of wood, brought together in your hands, could make a beautifully carved work of art, or something useful like a walking stick.

Remember, necessity is the mother of invention; life has shown us that all through the ages. Art is one example of that variety and invention, with paintbrushes and mark-makers created from the finest sable, to sticks broken off a bush in a backyard, and credit cards used as palette knives. I often use old credit cards or pieces of cut up plastic as mark makers in paintings. I've even used bubble wrap and the tread from a shoe sole. Sculptures can be made from junk lying around in a backyard or roadside. I remember one day seeing the most beautiful paintings done on some old cardboard cartons because the artist couldn't afford canvas to paint on; that didn't stop him, he painted on what he had available.

As far as tools or other necessities that may be needed in order to try something – many of us have a mindset that says, "It's too expensive, what if I spend the money and find I'm not good at it, or don't like it?" You need to know this – you are worth spending the money on in order to explore your creativity and see where it takes you. At the same time, don't think you have to persevere at something you don't like just because you paid money for supplies and tools for that endeavor; you can always sell them on your local Internet trading post (eBay or similar).

Measuring Success or Failure

Looking to see whether you are a success or failure at creativity is self-defeating. Living a full and enriched life is to take part in a process of learning and growing. I can remember holding a conversation with God about it one day as He challenged me to think again about the role of success and failure in my own life and the way I measured myself by them. He gave me a very simple definition of both when He explained that, in the end, "as a human, success is deemed to have happened when something turns out the way you hope or expect it to, and failure is when it doesn't." How true is that! Expectations and perspective play such a part in how we see things in life. When something works out how we expect it to, we deem it a success, and when it doesn't, we deem it a failure. And how often do we judge ourselves to be a success or failure in the same manner – when something turns out right we consider ourselves successful, and when it doesn't, we judge ourselves as failures.

Later that week the Lord and I continued our chat on success and failure, and He gave me the following prophetic encouragement, which has since blessed many hundreds of people.

"Taking two steps backwards after taking one forwards – maybe that's not failure, maybe it's part of a dance. Life is not a

linear journey; it's not moving forward in a straight line inexorably toward your goals. Looking at it that way produces the, 'Am I going forwards or backwards right now?' 'Taking ground or losing ground?' type of thinking, especially when something unexpected shifts plans and even goal posts. Think of life differently – maybe life is really like a divine dance, sometimes a step forward, sometimes two backwards, sometimes one to the side but always with you and Me moving together, making something beautiful out of the music provided by life's sounds, unheard frequencies, and happenings. In the midst of your shopping trip, your business affairs, your home life – allow yourself to get caught up in the beauty of the dance. I will lead you in the dance and I will help you to move in time to the eternal song being sung over your life. You may not hear that song, but the music is happening, and the song is being sung over you; so you might as well dance to it."   –Papa God

How to measure yourself in a healthy way

Success and failure are things we often measure ourselves by, but they are bad measuring sticks. A better measuring stick is to ask healthy questions such as...

- "How can I grow from this experience?"
- "What have I learned – about myself, about others, and about life?"
- "What things could I do differently next time?"
- "What things could I set in place in my life to help me not fall into that (way of thinking or behavioral) trap again?"

We all make mistakes or fail at times, but that does not make us failures. Give yourself a break; you don't have to prove that you have a good reason for existing by being the best or by succeeding (whatever that means to you). You are created in God's image and He loves you, whether you succeed or fail; that's what you truly need to know.

Creativity Activator

- Look over the list of creative pursuits found in this chapter, and write down any of the things that appeal to you and you would like to try out.

- Choose the one that appeals to you most of all – the one you would like to try first. Begin to check out how you can become involved in exploring that area of creativity. Look up classes online and sign up for one, or find out what you need to get started, and do so. Don't put it off; if you do you'll be less likely to actually try it out.

- Ask the Lord to come with you as you explore this new area of creativity – He loves spending time with you and He will encourage your creativity.

Chapter Six

The Creative Process

The creative process is not something you turn on and off; it's a part of life itself. It's how you make the life you are living. It's how you make anything!

Creating something is a process, not a sudden materialization. In saying that, most of you will think, "Of course, I know that." But often we see the end result of someone's creativity and forget the process of experimentation, learning and work that it took to get there. We see an end product and think that we could never create something like that, but if you know the process of creating, and you're willing to work that process, then you can see your ideas come into reality.

Making time for the process of creativity is crucial in order to get maximum benefits from the creative life. People process things in different ways and there are no right or wrong ways for doing so, but whatever way you choose to process, allotting sufficient time is important to get the maximum benefit from it.

Allocating merely ten minutes for the creative process before you rush out the door to start your day won't allow your creativity to flourish fully.

There is a process that most people go through when they're working toward the realization of an idea, and for most of us it is often unconscious. This process happens whether it's in creating a piece of art, a world-changing invention, or an idea that will revolutionize the way you do something at work.

Sometimes just knowing that this process exists, and that you are in it, is enough to get you through to the next stage. It's sometimes essential and comforting to be able to tell yourself, "This is part of the process, and I will get through it."

The Process of Creating

There are many different opinions on how many stages there are to the creative process, and everyone describes them differently. Most, however, agree on the most common stages, which are the ones I will cover in the following list. These stages aren't set in concrete, and are certainly not intended to be a formula; they're simply observations of the process. You may miss some of them, or you may go back and forwards a few times. Sometimes the creative process happens very quickly, other times it can take a while; yet the stages mentioned below are usually a part of that process. How long the process is doesn't matter, but recognizing where you are in the process does help.

- **Desire to create, or problem recognition** – This is where you're aware that you want to create something, or you know that a problem needs to be solved. In this stage you ask yourself, or others, questions to define the desire, or problem, and you begin to seek a solution.

- **Dream** – This is the "possibility" stage – you are thinking possibilities, but nothing more. It's the fun stage where everything is still possible and ideas flow from one to another. Write them all down, no matter how silly they seem to your rational mind. While you may settle on one idea to develop, you've now got a record of others that you can refer back to, especially in times of "creative block" when you want to create but can't think of ideas.

- **The "Aha" moment** – At this stage, you get a breakthrough idea. This "Aha" moment often comes when you are doing something unrelated to your project, yet your subconscious has been quietly working on it all the time. There are often feelings of joy and excitement as you envisage your idea. By all means savor them, but don't rely on them; those feelings will fade as you hit the other stages, and you will then have to believe in your idea and your capabilities, rather than rely on feelings. This stage can happen again many times, later in the process, as you work through the actual manifestation of your idea, from good idea to concrete reality.

- **Verification** – This stage is when you think the idea through to determine whether or not it could work. If the idea is plausible, then you move forward; if it's not, then you go back to dreaming again.

- **Research** – In this stage, you begin to find out exactly what's needed to meet that need. It's a time where you begin to gather information and do the research required; it's a time of questions, sifting, and answers to those questions. This stage may happen later in the process, too, as you hit snags and need to research new possibilities and answers.

- **Beginning to create** – In this stage you've assembled what you need and you begin to execute your idea. Excitement spurs you onward and you experience both delight and apprehension; delight, because you are starting to create, and apprehension, because you wonder if you have what it takes. At this stage the creative process carries you until you hit a problem, you realize how long the idea will take to complete, or you begin to doubt your ability.

- **Doubt** – The doubt stage is where your logical mind kicks in and tells you all the possible reasons why this isn't such a good idea after all. You may doubt your ideas and, possibly, even yourself. Remind yourself that the creative process is an adventure, and your identity does not depend on this idea working. That way you will be able to see more clearly without emotions clouding things. It's vitally important to divorce your identity from the process and the project. Otherwise, you will have a hard time creating. This is absolutely critical to really understand! You are not what you do. The project is simply something you are creating, it is not you.

- **Hard work** – This time is probably the most tedious – it's the "I want it finished now" stage! It may seem like it's never going to come together. There may even seem to be a lack of progress, but do not give up; you will get through it if you don't back down.

- **Inevitable problems** – This is really part of the "hard work" stage, but I wanted to mention it because it will happen – inevitably there will be problems along the way. It can be a time of both frustration and breakthrough, anger and doubt, but, all the while, you are making progress. This is not the time to pull back. Don't give up – you are nearly there!

- **Strategic determination** – Here is where you become even more strategic in what you do. You're purposeful in calling on your ability and training to accomplish the idea. This is where you know that you *can* do it and *will* do it.

- **It's finished** – It's here. Your idea is now reality – it's that "Aaahh" moment when you've put the finishing touch to it, step back and see it in its manifested gloriousness! You may feel quite euphoric and emotional, and at that moment all the things you went through in the process are worth it. This can be a vulnerable time, especially if you have a tendency to allow the project to become wrapped up in your identity. Don't allow this to happen; keep them separate! That way, when people criticize it, as some possibly will, you will not be as likely to think that they are criticizing you as a person.

I think that every person I know has gone through these stages as they've created things. Many times the creative process happens smoothly with little interruption and few problems. Other times many problems may need to be solved along the way, and it can be a battle to actually finish it. Sometimes a project can be emotionally uplifting; sometimes it can be hard emotionally! As I said earlier, just knowing where you are in the process can often be a help to getting you through to the end of it.

Life's creative process

The creative process we go through when doing a project of some sort is actually the same as the creative process we go through as we work on our lives. Whether it's growth in skills, character issues, or changing the way we see things, the same creative process happens.

How often have I dreamed of an area I longed to develop in my life, researched how best to do that, made progress, then doubted or hit a problem and stopped in the process until I could again find within me the strength and determination to continue. Other times I've hit a "speed bump," balked, and backed out of the process altogether, thinking, "This is just too hard," and in backing out, I haven't grown in that area until I've been willing to look at it again and continue in process. Yet all the while, it has been working toward what will become the finished work of art – my life.

We get to co-create our life with the Lord. We dream of what our life could look like, or maybe we get a prophetic word spoken over us, and we step into the process. We ask what we need to become that person, what tools, what character changes, and what help. We start out, but it's not long before doubt begins to attack us, or we hit a "speed bump." At this point we either give up, thinking it's too hard, that we were never made for this, or we go back to the drawing board, ask for strategy and continue. Then one day we'll stand at the end of our life, knowing that we've been responsible for co-creating with God this original masterpiece which is our life.

When we look at our life, we see not just one process but many, happening simultaneously, and we are often at different stages in the process for each part of our life. We are so complex, yet the same creative process is happening, whether in business, family life, personal growth or creativity. Multiple creative processes can be happening within our life at the same time, each producing something that goes toward the completion of the finished work. We are truly fearfully and wonderfully made!

THE CREATIVE PROCESS

 ## Creativity Activator 1

- Have a look at some of your past creative endeavors – see if you can recognize any of these stages in those projects. Then, as another activation, look back over your life and see where you can recognize the creative process at work in your life.

- Journal how you felt as you looked back over your projects, or your life, and how you think the understanding received from this chapter will be of help in future times and projects.

- If you have any projects that you've sidelined, you may want to get them out, dust them off and look at where you're up to in the process with them. Maybe you'll get some further inspiration that will enable you to move forward on them.

- Consider writing out the headlines of this process to pin on the wall where you do your creating, as a reminder, for when you're in the middle of doing something, that you will go through the process and you will come out on the other side.

 ## Creativity Activator 2

- **Make an ideas board** – It is a wonderful creativity activator. Buy a cork board, decorate it or leave it plain – that's up to you. Put it somewhere where you'll see it often. Now begin to pin onto it any ideas you have, or things that move or inspire you – words, pictures, and photos that move you, bits of cloth, photos of workspaces or rooms you like, art ideas you want to try, etc. Putting these things on your board puts the ideas where you can see them and allows your mind to subconsciously begin to dwell on them. This unconscious thought will eventually blossom into a moment of clarity, when you get the inspiration needed to begin a project.

Chapter Seven

Develop Your Creativity Further

Your creativity will not look like someone else's, and it doesn't have to. Stay true to who you are.

Your creative abilities, skills and gifts can be developed and broadened even further than what you are currently experiencing. In this chapter we're going to look at ways you can do this.

Most of us don't spend much time thinking about our creativity because the creative process usually happens automatically. In fact, it happens best when we aren't concentrating on trying to be creative. Creativity is an instinctive process for most of us and it often bypasses analytical thinking. That's why it's possible to be incredibly creative and still not recognize it – because it's so instinctive.

Creativity doesn't usually come fully formed – it comes as a seed within us at birth that we must nurture and develop. Often we look at others and marvel at how creative they are, and we forget that they weren't necessarily born like that; they actually had to develop their creativity. Even child prodigies still have to develop what they are given in order to grow and become even better than they are. I remember looking at the website of child prodigy artist Akiane Kramarik,[7] marveling at her skill and ability, and seeing how much her gift developed as she grew. Even though she was recognized as a child prodigy in the areas of art and poetry, her gifts were developed through putting them into practice, the same way that we all develop.

There is definitely a process that happens as we grow and develop our creative skills and abilities. We start with the desire to try something, and we give it a go. Sometimes we turn out something worth keeping and sometimes we don't, but we will never know what we are fully capable of in any given area unless we are willing to spend time developing the skillsets needed. Developing your creativity is like developing any other skillset that you have. There are tools you can use to help you in the growth process, and there are exercises you can do to strengthen and enhance your abilities. The main key lies in you believing that it can happen, and then setting out to make it happen.

Tips for developing your creativity

There are many things that you can do to enhance and grow your creativity. Here are some ideas to help you further develop it.

- **Give yourself permission to be creative** – This is really important. So many of us have been brought up to believe that time spent being creative is wasted time. This is not true! Creativity is the seedbed for all new ideas and the advancement of society and culture. You need to be

---
[7] Akiane Kramarik - https://art-soulworks.com/pages/akiane-art-gallery

creative; if you are not, you'll shut down and die on the inside in so many ways – life will become a drudgery, something to get through instead of something to live to its fullest. Give yourself permission to be creative – it will help feed your soul and give it life!

- **Commit yourself to developing your creativity** – This inner commitment will actually become one of your values. Our values drive our decisions, so there must be that inner commitment for any outworking to happen consistently. This decision can be as simple as resolving that you are going to give it priority, or it can be as structured as setting aside specific time to do exercises that develop your creative abilities.

- **Make time for creativity** – Like all abilities, your creativity won't develop to its fullest if it's not nurtured, with designated time for it. Do try to schedule regular time for creative projects, but don't become rigid and legalistic about it.

- **Put aside preconceived ideas** – When we go to solve a problem or be creative, any preconceived ideas may hem us in. Put them aside and allow your thoughts free rein.

- **Put aside judgment and self-criticism** – These will lock down and block creativity. Don't judge your creative efforts against other people's – it's not a competition (unless you enter a formal competition; and then it's important to remember – any judge's opinion is simply that – their opinion. It is what they think – maybe their personal preferences and their beliefs based on technical expertise).

- **Understand that creativity is a "whole brain" thing** – Contrary to popular belief, creativity is not connected to one side of the brain only. The two different sides of our brain are creative in different ways, each side of the brain triggering different ways of thinking. The left side of our brain is said to be more logical, analytical and objective. The right side of the brain is said to be more intuitive, thoughtful and subjective. They each use creativity to solve problems and create things, but they just approach it from different angles. Neither is better than the other, and the best creativity will happen when both sides are used together.

- **Allow yourself to be curious** – Curiosity is hugely important to creativity. "What ifs" are the doorways to incredible potential. Curiosity leads to discovery, potential answers and creative fulfillment. Don't scold yourself for being curious and asking questions. Ask more! It's the curious, often unreasonable, person who gets results. What do I mean by that? It's the person who pushes, who asks questions, who won't accept the first "No" as their limit, that makes things happen, and curiosity is the start of that process.

- **Give yourself permission to take risks** – Taking risks is an important part of growth – in fact, no growth happens without risk. Your risks may not pay off every time, but they're an important part of developing your creative abilities.

- **Embrace the importance of the process** – Recognize that the creative process has its own rewards and is just as important as creative fulfillment.

- **Target negative thoughts, attitudes, and emotions** – Be intentional about this; choose to target them and turn them into positive thoughts. Develop your ability to stay in a positive state of mind and maintain positive emotions as much as possible – your mood will affect your creativity, and creativity usually happens best when you're in a positive state of mind.

- **Generate as many ideas as you can** – There's never just one answer or solution to a problem; there can be multiple solutions. Recognize that the first solution you come up with is not always the best. Thinking up multiple solutions will help develop your ability to think creatively.

- **Allow yourself to be messy** – Give yourself permission to be free and to make a mess. Learn to create in a non-calculated way. See where it takes you and how free you feel. You should aim to become totally unselfconscious in your creativity, and this won't happen if you are always censoring yourself and making yourself tidy things up. Don't allow your censoring adult mind to inhibit your creativity and therefore place limits on yourself.

- **Experiment and play** – Deliberately take time to experiment and play. Give yourself permission to do so without your creating having to be for a particular purpose; play is a valid purpose in itself. Explore new techniques and styles; push your personal limits as to what is acceptable. Don't censor or restrict your creativity – allow it to be stretched. Trying something doesn't commit you to keeping it. Don't box yourself in by having to produce; allow yourself time to play. When it comes to art in particular, you can always use your play stuff as backgrounds or ideas for later creative endeavors.

- **Allow yourself to make mistakes** – Many wonderful creative things have come out of a so-called "mistake." I've heard it said that mistakes are just your creativity taking its own path, so let it do that; follow it and see where it goes. Mistakes are not bad, and they are not failures; every mistake is an opportunity to learn and to find a different way to do something.

- **Give yourself permission to have "downtime"** – Many people feel that they're somehow wasting time and being unproductive if they allow themselves time to sit and reflect. There is such pressure in society today to achieve, to have a "performance-based" mentality, or to be "on the go" all the time, yet it's critical to the creative process to make time to sit quietly. Give yourself permission to do so. At first your mind will war with it, but if you don't give in, it will soon accept this as part of your routine.

- **Keep a notebook handy** – List ideas as they occur. Don't rely on your ability to remember them later; you usually won't. I carry a notebook in my handbag and have paper beside my computer for writing thoughts on.

- **Don't let yourself get bogged down** – Sometimes we can get bogged down (i.e., we spend so much time thinking about something that we can't think clearly any longer). Take your mind off your project or problem and allow your subconscious to work on it while you do something else. Lots of things have been solved through "Aha" moments that have come as the person was doing something else. Solutions and ideas can even come while you're asleep. Many problems have been solved and invented because of dreams.

- **Brainstorm** – When you start a new project, take time to brainstorm. Write whatever comes to mind when you think about the project, then let your mind run wild – write down as many ideas as possible. Remember, at this stage in a project there are no silly, right or wrong ideas; just ideas. The sifting will come later. In Lewis Carroll's book, *Alice in Wonderland*, Alice quotes her father and says, "Why, sometimes I've believed as many as six impossible things before breakfast." Allow yourself to dream and generate ideas; don't try to play safe with them. "Impossible" is not a word to contemplate, and impossible is only ever an opinion anyway; many things we once thought impossible are now in everyday use.

- **Broaden your outlook** – Read books, trawl the Internet, listen to music, go to a library, museum, or art gallery. Challenge your habitual ways of thinking or doing things, and your current limitations. Look at a variety of different options – don't just stick with stuff you like.

- **Don't be afraid of getting inspiration from others** – Most creative people use other people's work to spark their own creativity at some point in their creative journey, and it's not a sign of failure to do so. Albert Einstein once said, "The secret to creativity is knowing how to hide your sources."

- **Be flexible** – It's too easy to get locked into our normal way of approaching a subject. Deliberately look for alternative ways of thinking about the subject. Be willing to consider different perspectives, ideas, and scenarios.

- **Deliberately fight fear of failure** – Fear of failure is the fear that you don't have what it takes – that somehow you are not good enough. This fear is a creativity killer. Remind yourself that all the best people fail and many of them failed many times before succeeding. Fear inhibits – it reins us in, as we try to make things perfect.

- **Learn to separate your work from your identity** – You are not what you do; your work is simply something you produce. People can dislike your work without disliking you. No doubt there are plenty of things your family and friends do that you dislike, but you still like them.

- **Learn to deal with rejection** – Even though people will reject your work at times, that doesn't mean they are rejecting or dismissing your value as a person. The fear of rejection, of other people not liking your work, will actually stop you from being as creative as you can be. On the plus side, rejection may have positive outcomes; it can force you to explore other ideas and look at developing yourself further. So don't listen to too much criticism. If listening for criticism of your work is what you automatically gravitate toward, it shows an unhealthy belief about yourself and your work. Don't let criticism affect you or ruin your belief in yourself.

- **Fight perfection and don't fuss** – Perfection is another one of the creativity killers. It's often the spontaneous thoughts or accidents that prove to be the most creative part of what we produce. Fussing will lead to tight and uninspiring work. Detail is fine if detail is called for, but perfectionism and fussing aren't the same as putting in needed detail. Don't lie to yourself and call yourself a detail person if you are in fact a fusser. Recognize it and teach yourself to let go; ask, "What am I afraid of that makes me a fusser?"

- **Evaluate correctly** – Learn to evaluate your work at a professional level, not at an identity level. For example, "I need to work on perspective – that road and the buildings don't end at the right vanishing point," rather than, "I knew I couldn't do this. I'm not good enough."

- **Learn to identify your strengths and weaknesses** – Learn what your hidden strengths are and what your permanent weaknesses are; the only way you can do this is to try something a few times. Over time, and with practice, some things may improve and become strengths; some things may not.

- **Choose to make things instead of buying them, where you can** – Creating something you need is not only very therapeutic, it gives you something handmade and preserves skills for future generations that could otherwise be lost. There is currently a worldwide rise in people doing crafts again as another generation finds the pleasure in creating something.

- **Keep your creative supplies handy** – Pens, pencils, paints, glue, wool and knitting needles, embroidery hoops and floss – keep the things that relate to your creativity handy. You need to be able to put your hands on them quickly; if you have to spend time searching for them, you're more likely to tell yourself that you can't be bothered.

- **Learn new things** – How the brain processes information, how color affects people, placement of objects, what different shapes do; for example, organic versus geometric. There is so much that we can learn that will help our creative endeavors to be successful.

- **Doodle** – Doodling is great for boosting creativity. It too often gets a bad rap, but it's a great aid to creativity – studies show it improves your concentration and comprehension, helps you think, helps with information processing, and improves creative thinking. Doodling while in a learning situation where someone is speaking involves all four learning modes (visual, auditory, reading/writing and kinesthetic) and causes a greater retention of information by over 25%, according to studies.[8] Look up "doodles," "zentangle"[9] and "sketchnoting"[10] on Google or whatever Internet search engine you use. Be inspired by where your doodles could take you. Doodle away and grow creatively!

Creativity Activator 1

Ask yourself these questions:

- In what ways do I counteract or sabotage my creativity?

- What's my self-talk like? Am I already making excuses for why it won't turn out how I want?

- Write down some of your most commonly used self-talk phrases like, "I bet I won't be any good at this," "This is not my thing," "I'm useless at this," "I don't have the skills needed," etc.

- Then write down a truth to counteract those phrases, e.g., "I bet I won't be good at this" becomes "I won't know if

---

[8] Time magazine article on doodling http://www.time.com/time/health/article/0,8599,1882127,00.html
Books/Websites with information on Doodling – The Doodle Revolution, Sunni Brown
Website – http://curkovicartunits.pbworks.com/w/page/29160521/Doodle%20Lab%20Club%20Activity

[9] Books/Websites with information on Zentangle – Joy of Zentangle – Marie Browning and Suzanne McNeill
Website – http://tanglepatterns.com/tips-tools/tutorials
or http://craftwhack.com/how-to-zentangle/

[10] Books/Websites with information on Sketchnotes – The Sketchnote Handbook – Mike Rohde
Website – http://www.smashingmagazine.com/2014/11/10/how-to-get-started-with-sketchnotes/

I'm good at this until I give it a go; it may be a hidden strength."

- You'll no doubt be your own greatest critic, but teach yourself to distinguish truth from fears. You'll find that a fear will usually be hiding underneath your excuses. Recognize and deal with the fear, and you'll find the freedom to "'have a go."

Now look at some areas of creativity that you want to develop:

- What areas of your creativity would you like to develop?
- What ways could you develop them? Are there classes you can take locally; are there instructional guides or websites you could check out?
- What do you need to resource yourself with in order to develop them – materials, tools, etc.?
- When and how are you going to start, or restart (if you had stopped developing in that area)?

 *Creativity Activator 2*

- Do some doodling, or, if you want your doodling to have a little more structure, try some zentangle. You may find doodling hard to begin with, especially if you have a tendency to think of it as "wasting time," but it is worth persevering with. As I've said earlier, it has great value and helps develop our creativity.

- Set aside some time to doodle each day for a week and see what happens. It may make you realize you need to re-think some of your beliefs regarding play, wasting time, what valuable creativity is, etc. If so, look at those beliefs honestly and see what limiting beliefs or lies you need to deal with.

Chapter Eight

Creativity in Later Life

You're never too old to learn something new or to try something you've never tried before.

Aging is something that happens to us all, yet it's also something very few of us look forward to. Everyone has ideas of what life is going to be like as they age, and society tends to reinforce those ideas, especially the negative ones. Media, TV, and Hollywood all play a big part in how we view aging.

Dismantling Stereotypes

On TV or in movies we see images that stereotype different groups of people and use those stereotypes so often that we begin to see all that group of people in a certain light – the computer geek, the workaholic CEO, lawyers, divorcees, the mentally ill, the disabled, and, of course, elderly people. In Western society, in particular, many people have been negatively influenced by media's portrayals of aging people.

Older people are too often shown in a negative light and are often portrayed as sitting around in "old folks' homes" staring at the walls, waiting for sickness or death to overtake them. Alzheimer's, dementia, strokes, broken hips, the need for dentures and adult diapers, all of these things are the subject of TV advertising aimed at people as they grow older, and often these things are even featured strongly in TV programs and movies. Yet, even though some of that may be a reality for a percentage of the aging population (but certainly doesn't take away their value), it does not give a true or balanced picture of growing older. Many people live full and healthy lives right up until the moment they die. We are also increasingly seeing people live longer lives; the average life expectancy in western civilization, in particular, has increased significantly over the past century.[11]

In Isaiah, God tells us that He will sustain us:

"Even to your old age and gray hairs I am He; I am He who will sustain you. I have made you and I will carry you; I will sustain you and I will rescue you."　　　*—Isaiah 46:4 NIV*

What an amazing promise from the Lord! *Sustain* means "to strengthen or support physically or mentally." God promises that even as we grow older He will strengthen and support both our physical and mental faculties. We can expect to live fulfilling lives right up until we go to be with Him. That applies to our creativity, too. He will sustain it – strengthen and support us in it. You don't have to lose your creative abilities as you grow older. Yes, some of the things you do, and the way you express your creativity, may change, but your creativity does not need to be lost.

---

[11] https://www.nia.nih.gov/research/publication/global-health-and-aging/living-longer

There are many people that society deems as "old" or "elderly" who live fulfilling, vibrant, passionate and creative lives. This book will help you to be one of those people!

The life-giving power of creativity in senior years

Creative expression has been proven to benefit us in every area of life, especially as we age. In his "Study on Creativity and Aging,"[12] Gene Cohen discovered that elderly people benefitted greatly from creative pursuits. He studied a group of 300 people ranging in age from 65 to 100, over a two year period. The study showed that those who were involved in creative pursuits found their overall health improved significantly in many areas, compared to those who did nothing creative. Physical and mental health, brain plasticity, medication usage, relationships, doctor visits, physical balance and falls, feelings of vibrancy and morale – all these things have been proven to benefit from a person expressing their creativity. In fact, living a creative life has been proven to give one a better quality of life in every area than living an uncreative one.

In Psalm 92:12-15 the Lord talks to us about the righteous man (or woman) and tells us this: *"They will still bear fruit in old age, they will stay fresh and green, proclaiming, "The* Lord *is upright; he is my Rock, and there is no wickedness in him."* NIV

You can expect to still be creative and bear fruit in old age, and being older gives you an advantage in many ways, one of which is found in Job 12:12, *"Wisdom belongs to the aged, and understanding to the old."* NLT

---

[12] Study on Creativity and Aging by Gene D Cohen, M.D. Ph.D.
https://cahh.gwu.edu/sites/cahh.gwu.edu/files/downloads/NEA_Study_Final_Report_0.pdf
http://www.peopleandstories.net/wp-content/uploads/2011/08/RESEARCH-ON-CREATIVITY-AND-AGING1.pdf

With age comes wisdom and understanding, so you can expect to understand things on a whole different level than a younger person who has far less life experience does. There is some understanding and wisdom that only comes with age and life experience. When we are younger, we often don't realize the value of the many gifts God has given us; we can tend to take them for granted, thinking that we will always have them. Yet, as we all know, we can take nothing for granted in life except the Lord's love and faithfulness.

Facing Restrictions

Aging can sometimes bring restrictions to our life – let's be realistic about that. Maybe you can't do the creative things you've always loved because of mobility issues or pain, but don't let that stop you. Seek out other creative pursuits that you can do. Look for ways around your restrictions. For example, if you're an artist and you can no longer do detailed controlled work, then try a more free and abstracted style of painting. Don't give up altogether; there are always ways around problems. Let your creativity loose and find a way!

Never Too Late

Creativity is one thing we so easily take for granted; we don't even think about it when we are younger, so we often don't intentionally guard and develop it. Even if you didn't guard and develop it when you were younger, it's not too late to develop it now.

It's never too late to learn new things or let your creativity loose. Who knows where that may lead you and what joys you'll discover!

As a child I was never very creative, apart from having a very fertile imagination. All my energy went into simply surviving.

But my imagination was my escape from a very difficult childhood. I didn't start to explore creative things until I was in my mid-twenties, when I discovered dance as an expression I could use in my worship of God. I never had dance lessons but it wasn't long before I was teaching worship dance in classes around the nation and people began asking me for teaching notes. I wrote and published my first book, *Praise Him in the Dance*, in my late 20s as a study guide for Church dance groups, simply because so many people asked me for teaching on that subject. I never thought of myself as a writer, it was simply something that was needed. Then life intervened, and I largely stopped writing as I focused on raising my family and becoming more involved in pastoral ministry.

While I did explore painting and some occasional writing over the intervening years, it wasn't until I was in my 40s that the desire to write grew within me and I began to really focus on writing again. And it wasn't until I was age 54 that my second book[13] was published. Since then my love for writing has exploded, and I've written numerous articles, books and training manuals, and discovered that writing is one of my chief joys in life.

My sister Marianne went to University in her mid-50s for the first time and graduated four years later with a bachelor's degree in Computer Graphic Design. During that time she found a new area of creativity within her that led to her setting up her own web and graphic design business at the age of 59.

Many people who were never really creative in earlier years have found previously unrealized and unreleased creativity in their later years, often becoming very successful and well known in their fields of endeavor.

---

[13] "Visions, Visitations and the Voice of God" by Lyn Packer published in 2010 by XP Publishing

More stories[14]

- Many writers have published their first major work later in life. Mary Wesley wrote two children's books in her late 50s, then in her 70s she published her first novel, and that's when her career as an author really took off.

- Harriet Doerr published her first novel, *Stones for Ibarra*, at the age of 74.

- Laura Ingalls Wilder became a journalist in her 40s, but it wasn't until she was in her 60s that she published the first novel in the *Little House* series of children's books. This series was later made into a popular television show, "Little House on the Prairie."

- Harry Bernstein's first book, *The Invisible Wall*, was written at age 94 and published at age 96.

- Edmond Hoyle was about age 70 when he began writing his books on the rules for card games. These books would become famous and establish him as one of the first technical writers.

- Grandma Moses began her painting career in her 70s after arthritis forced her to stop doing the embroidery she loved. She is well known for her simple style and rural scenes. Her art became so popular that her name is recognized worldwide.

---

[14] These stories of peoples' creativity have been collected by myself over many years from various sources; sadly, along the way I lost some of the original sources that I gained that information from, but was able to confirm all of it from various Internet sources, such as: http://en.wikipedia.org/wiki/Late_bloomer
http://www.ehayes.co.nz/Hayes-Motorworks-Collection/Burt-Munro-__I.5
http://www.thefamouspeople.com/profiles/colonel-sanders-3728.php
http://www.biography.com/people/grandma-moses-9416251#synopsis

- Bill Traylor started drawing at age 83 or so and went on to produce approximately 1,500 pieces of art.

- Alfred Wallis began painting in his 60s. His naïve or simplistic style captured many things from his lifetime that would otherwise have been forgotten, such as certain landmarks and types of ships.

- Frieda Lefeber is someone who knows it's never too late. Now 101, Frieda had her first ever solo art exhibit when she was 100 years old. Frieda began taking art classes at age 76 and earned a degree from the Pennsylvania Academy of the Fine Arts at age 83. "I had no idea I could paint," she said. Frieda published her autobiography when she was 88.

- Colonel Sanders began his Kentucky Fried Chicken franchise in his 60s and became a huge success with franchises worldwide. You might wonder what Colonel Sanders is doing in a list of creative people, considering he was a businessman. The two are not mutually exclusive; it took creativity to develop and expand his business, as well as to create the blend of herbs and spices that he used to coat his chicken – that was creative genius at work.

- At the age of 52, Carol Gardner was newly divorced, broke and depressed. Yet from that place she went on to establish a greeting card company, Zelda Wisdom (inspired by her English bulldog), now worth over $50 million dollars.

- Irene Wells Pennington took over the family business in her 90s after her husband became sick, and became well known for her business expertise.

- In his mid-fifties, Taikichiro Mori founded a building and real estate empire in Japan that made him the richest man in the world during the early 1990s. He came from a merchant family, but he had been a business professor before his 50s.

- At age 89, Barbara Beskind got a job she loves – as an industrial designer. Barbara, now 91, draws from her many years of experience as an occupational therapist to work with engineers on products that improve the quality of life for older people.

- Josh Scharf, 62, an industrial designer, creates smart-living products for baby boomers, such as automatic light systems for stairs/pathways to help people see better at night and prevent falls. John Calvert, the executive director of the United Inventors Association, said, "There's a boom in inventions by people over 50. Over 60% of the association's members are older, so they have more time for inventing."

- In New Zealand, a man named Burt Munro had a dream to create the fastest motorcycle in the world. With a lot of creativity, hard work, and belief in his idea, in spite of others openly laughing and discouraging him, he set to work to modify his motorbike engine and tune it so it could reach its top possible speed. Putting his creativity to work, he designed and made parts – often using old tins and whatever else he could find to work with. Eventually, at the age of 68, Burt Munro took his Indian motorbike to the Bonneville Salt Flats in 1967. The result – a land speed record that still holds today, over fifty years later. His creative and literal journey was later immortalized in the film "The World's Fastest Indian."

 *Creativity Activator*

- Set aside some time to sit, reflect, and dream. Look back over your life and acknowledge your life journey and your journey in creativity. Don't judge it; just accept that this has been your journey up until now. Allow no self-recrimination, and no internal or verbal judgment, about your journey so far. If you need to, forgive any people that quashed your creativity, including yourself. Come to peace with where you are now regarding your creativity, and realize that you get to start again from this moment. The past is the past, whether good or bad, but the past does not have to dictate your future.

- Write a journal entry relating to this, describing what your creativity was like as a child, and what happened to it as you grew. Share about how being creative or losing creativity made you feel, and the effects it had on your life. Be honest; no one is going to read this except you (unless you choose to share it with others).

- Now begin to allow yourself to dream of what your creative future could look like. What sort of life do you want to create? What sort of creative life do you want to live? Give yourself permission to start again, putting the negative things of the past behind you. Ask God to help you as you step into this next phase of life. Ask Him to help you develop your creativity; it's never too late to do so. What areas of creativity do you feel drawn to? You may not have definite ideas at this stage, but by the end of this book I'm sure you will.

Chapter Nine

Developing a Culture of Creativity

Part of being creative is breaking out of established thinking patterns and daring to create new roads where others may follow.

We live in a world where our lives are affected by culture every day – our family culture, peer cultures, national cultures, church cultures and more. The influence of culture plays a huge part in our lives in relation to how we see and react to our world. If you grow up in a family or culture where creativity is quashed or derided, then you will tend to repress your creative instincts. If you grow up in a culture where creativity is celebrated, you are more likely to be open to using or developing your creativity.

Society, in general, and the school system, in particular, does not openly encourage creativity, and as a result we are the poorer for it. It's time to do something about that, and the best place to begin is with your own life. Look at how you can intentionally begin to develop a culture of creativity in your personal, family or church life. It's time to become deliberate about creating a culture in our lives, schools, and workplaces that openly celebrates, encourages, explores, and develops creativity.

How to develop a culture of creativity

How can we develop a culture of creativity in our homes, schools and churches, and how can we use the creativity God has given us to encourage, inspire and help our communities? There are some ways listed below, but I'm sure that you will be able to come up with others, also.

- **Be intentional.** Creativity will not flourish unless we are intentional about creating an environment where it is free to do so. That means making a place in our minds, as well as in our church culture and meetings, for creativity to have a part.

- **Recognize and promote the reality that everyone is creative.** Talk about it; encourage people to find their creative expression – whether in the workplace, at home, or in creative leisure pursuits.

- **Recognize that everyone has ideas.** Everyone is creative. Don't prejudge people or judge them on beginning efforts. Who knows, you may have the next Akaine Kramarik in your congregation, waiting to be encouraged and let loose to create masterpieces.

- **Recognize the power of symbols and creativity to communicate.** Symbols have long been used to communicate, both in society and in the Church. The cross is a great example of that and is recognized globally as being the symbol of Christianity. How can you use symbols and creativity to communicate – to your church, to the community, in church documents, in worship and advertising, etc.?

- **Teach on what Scripture says** – about creativity and imagination, and their place in our lives.

- **Showcase talents and creative expressions.** One church near us has a few artists in their congregation and they regularly display and rotate artworks on their sanctuary and hall walls for people to enjoy and gain insight from. You could hold Easter or Christmas-related exhibitions, like a "Stations of the Cross" interactive walk-through exhibition at Easter, giving your artists, sculptors, potters, engineers and carpenters total freedom to create art pieces for the community to experience. What about a "clean up your beach/park" day with artists creating on-the-spot works out of the trash, and other artworks on display, as well? You could also have free face painting for the kids, a barbeque, and make it a family day out. The possibilities are endless.

- **Encourage creative thinking.** Don't settle for mediocre or the first solution offered. Push for more ideas and brainstorm – allow time to do so without the fear of it being unproductive time. Especially when brainstorming, there are no silly ideas. That so-called silly idea might just be the answer to a problem or spark the idea that is needed.

- **Offer structure for freedom of expression.** People will feel safer trying something new if they're not left to flounder along on their own. Classes, as well as places to experiment, can often give support when trying new things. For example, you could set up art tables at the back of the room where people can create visual expressions during worship.

- **Provide opportunities for creative expression.** What are ways you can make room for creative expression? What groups or classes could you offer your church or community? How can you use creative expressions in worship times, etc.?

- **Encourage trying.** Create a culture where it's okay to "give it a go" – where it's okay to try something to see if you like it or have an aptitude for it.

- **Embrace failure.** Let people know it's not only okay to fail, but failing is part of the growth process. Teach them how to benefit and learn from their failures. Teach them tenacity, and instill in them that "go again" and "don't give up" mindset.

- **Create an active support system.** Provide encouragement and support for innovators, who are found in every sector of society – business, government, media, arts and entertainment, education, the family, and religion (plus many subgroups under these main categories).

- **Collaborate.** Encourage collaboration. Wonderful things happen in collaboration. New ideas are sparked, ideas get tweaked and improved upon, and more can be achieved when we work together.

- **Use new technology.** Don't stay stuck in the Dark Ages; embrace new technologies and use them. While not every technology will be suitable for your situation, many of them are. For example, use social media to communicate – take advantage of the freedom we have with Facebook, Instagram, Twitter, etc. If you don't know how to use them, get training.[15] Invest in your personal life, your team, your church, your community. Take advantage of what is available.

---

[15] Patricia King Ministries offers a training course in using social media such as Facebook; you can find out more here – http://pki.xpmedia.com/p/social-media-made-simple

- **Open up the innovation process and platform.** Don't restrict it to the few who have already been acknowledged as creative. I know it can seem easier to rely on the same few people, but if you do you may very well get stuck in the creative rut of their thinking and limitations. Open it up; let others have a go at it. Let that 12-year-old video whiz create a piece of filmwork to bless others. Allow that grandmother to teach young mothers how to balance work and home life creatively – both will be blessed by it, and intergenerational relationships will blossom.

- **Reach out.** Use your creative skills as an individual and as a group to touch and bless your community. Offer classes – in art, cooking, job skills, mothering skills, car maintenance, basic DIY skills/projects, dance classes, etc. Hold Easter art exhibitions or drama productions, family "day out" events, or Christmas productions. There are so many possibilities and ways that the creative skills in your congregation can be utilized and expressed to bless the community around you.

These are just a few ways in which we can encourage and promote the use of creativity in our churches and communities. Start a discussion with your church about how you can use creativity more in your community, both within and outside the church, then determine to do something to help your church reach its creative potential.

Creativity in Church History

Culture has always played a great part in steering society, and the culture of the Church is no exception. As we've seen earlier, God loves and celebrates creativity, and for many years the Church did, too, until wrong thinking came in and repression took over.

In the early church it was common to see expressions of dance, both individual and group, spontaneous and choreographed. Justin Martyr (AD 150) and Hippolytus (AD 200) describe in their writings how dance was used to worship God; both men describe joyful circle dances in the sanctuary. In the early fourth century, Eusebius, "the father of church history," wrote a detailed account of the dancing in a particular worship service that was both spontaneous and choreographed. Countless other church leaders also spoke or wrote approvingly of dance as an expression of worship.

Spontaneous and prewritten songs were a regular part of the worship expression. As we've seen earlier in this book, Scripture clearly tells us that both spontaneous and written songs were encouraged by the Lord and used congregationally. The chorus/stanza type of song developed in the early church as it entered the Middle Ages. The word "chorus" comes from the Greek word *choros*, meaning "to dance, dancing, an enclosure for dance." The Greek word *stanza* means "to stand." Dancers commonly stood still during the stanza and danced during the chorus. The word *choir* originally meant "a band of dancers and singers." Thus, many of our early hymns and Christmas carols were written with the idea of danced expression in mind.

Instruments, while openly encouraged and used in Scripture and the early Church in expressing worship, were forbidden in Church-use for many centuries. That's where the Gregorian chants of the monks originated; all they had to use were their voices. It's only been in the last century or so that instruments have become acceptable in worship again. In the early part of that resurgence, only organ and, later, piano, were acceptable, with the exception of the Salvation Army brass bands. Even as late as the 1980s, instruments such as guitars, drums and other such instruments were frowned upon in many places. It's really only been in the last forty to fifty years that we have seen the majority of the churches accept such expressions of creativity in worship.

Martin Luther, that great reformer, had much to say about music. Here are some of his more famous quotes:

Next to the Word of God, the noble art of music is the greatest treasure in the world.

Beautiful music is the art of the prophets that can calm the agitations of the soul; it is one of the most magnificent and delightful presents God has given us.

The devil, the originator of sorrowful anxieties and restless troubles, flees before the sound of music almost as much as before the Word of God. Music is a gift and grace of God, not an invention of men. Thus it drives out the devil and makes people cheerful. Then one forgets all wrath, impurity, and other devices.

For many years, Martin Luther's voice was one of only a few that spoke in defense of the arts in church culture.

Throughout the ages, the Church recognized the power of art to inspire people and to proclaim the gospel, and they used it to great effect – not just for decoration in their cathedrals but to tell the story of God's relationship with mankind and to teach scriptural principles. Yet that expression also saw a period of hundreds of years where it was not encouraged. Artworks were even destroyed in many churches because art was believed by many to be anti-scriptural and in violation of the Ten Commandments. Over the centuries, in nations where religious repression happened, many thousands of altarpieces and artworks were destroyed and lost forever. But in the last ten to twenty years, art has again become a part of many church's worship expression, with artists doing prophetic artworks during the worship that express what is on the heart of God for that congregation.

For many centuries the majority of the population of Europe and England weren't educated, and therefore couldn't read or write, so the Church often used drama to proclaim the gospel message. In the early Middle Ages in England and Europe, they would drive pageant wagons to different places, and priests and monks would act out the major gospel messages. They still hold huge Easter pageants to this day in some European cities.

In what has become known as the Dark Ages, many of the Church's creative expressions were repressed and lost. It wasn't until the Reformation that creativity began to be expressed again in the Church. But even then, many people refused to accept that creativity was a gift from God; they viewed it as evil and worldly. It has only been since the 20th century that the Church has again begun to recognize creativity as a gift from God imparted to mankind in His creation of them. Even with that recognition happening, though, it has been a long battle to get the church globally to accept creative expressions as part of their worship again.

Obviously, there is so much more to the history of creative expression in the church, and I haven't even scratched the surface of it. Why don't you do some research yourself, if this topic interests you? There are many great books[16] that deal with the subject of art and creativity within the Church.

Creativity in the Church today

The Church should be the place where creativity is celebrated, recognized, encouraged and cultivated the most. Our churches

---

[16] Some books on the arts and creativity in Christianity - Art Needs No Justification – H R Rookmaaker; Born to Create – Theresa Dedmon; Art and the Bible – Francis Schaeffer

should be full of people who know how to express their creativity in every area of life and, in doing so, bless the communities they are part of.

As Christians we should be more creative than anyone. Why? Because not only do we have the creativity God gifted to us when He created mankind, but we also have relationship with the Trinity. These three – Father, Son, and Holy Spirit – are the creators of all things; we have been given access to their help through our relationship with them, and have been given empowerment through the mind of Christ and the help of the Holy Spirit.

But we have the mind of Christ. —*1 Corinthians 2:16*

"But I tell you the truth, it is to your advantage that I go away; for if I do not go away, the Helper will not come to you; but if I go, I will send Him to you." —*John 16:7*

"…The Holy Spirit, whom the Father will send in My name, He will teach you all things…" —*John 14:26*

The Church should be leading the way in creative expression and invention and, while we are making up lost ground, we still have a long way to go before we are back to where the Lord intends us to be. We need to be discussing how we can again celebrate and promote creativity in all its varieties in our church communities, and actively championing the development of it. Think about ways that you can do this…

 ## Creativity Activator

- Get a group of people together to talk about creativity and come up with ideas for a way forward. Think about, and discuss with others, the ways in which you can develop a culture and practice of creativity in your church or group.

- Discuss the place of creativity currently in your church or group – this is not a judgment time, but it is an honest assessing. Remember, you can't change something until you look at it honestly and come up with ideas that can help change things.

- Don't moan if there is no room at present for creative expression in your church; moaning doesn't change things. Be proactive, come up with ideas and suggestions for a way forward, then present those suggestions in a loving manner to your leadership, and open up a place for dialogue and progress to happen.

- Make a list of activities or groups that you could start in your church to promote creativity within the lives of the church members.

- Discuss how you can use the creative talent within your church to help and encourage the community around you. Look at the talent and skills within your church family and think of classes or groups that would be a blessing to your community.

Chapter Ten

More Creativity Activators

Take time to be creative every day. Make things of beauty and usefulness; life will be the richer for doing so.

There's something really pleasurable about the process of creating, and I want you to experience that in as many ways as possible, so this chapter is full of ideas to try that will develop your creativity in new ways.

Most of us have preferences and certain ways we look at things and, while that's not necessarily wrong, it can cause us to think in a limited fashion, which can sometimes cause our creative works to have a feeling of sameness about them. On a positive side, that sameness can be what causes people to recognize our work from someone else's – it's our style. But on a negative front, if the sameness comes from limited thinking, then we won't produce inspired and varied work.

Maybe that "sameness" comes because we can't think of what to do, and where to start, so we turn to what we already know how to do. That's where these activations can help.

Below are 31 different ideas you could try that will stretch you to think in new and different ways. That's an idea a day for a whole month, if you want to go that route. Most of them can be done multiple times. As you do them, each time you'll come up with something completely different from the time before. There is no end to your creativity, and these activations will help you see that to a greater degree than ever.

Each of the activations below will have the effect of expanding your creative abilities; they will help you think outside the box of your normal preferences and will make you look at things with new eyes.

1. **Create an activation box.** Print out these activations, and others, onto cardboard, cut them up to separate them from each other, and put them in a box. Decorate the box and label it something like: "Creativity Boosters," "Activation box," "Prompt box," "Inspiration," "Kickstarter." When you find inspiration lacking, then draw one of the activations out and use it to inspire your creativity.

2. **Pictures that move you.** Look through old magazines and cut or tear out pictures or words that move you in some way. They can be happy, sad, cute, make you angry, disconcert you, make you smile, laugh, etc. Stick them in an envelope in the back of your journal or in a file you keep in your creating space. Use them in your artwork, let them inspire you

MORE CREATIVITY ACTIVATORS

or illustrate what you are writing about in your journal. Use them as a stand-alone entry, letting them become the focus of that whole creativity time. You can also do this as a focused activation over a specific time period – do it for a couple of weeks or a month, picking a new picture each day. Then see if there is a common thread to the pictures. Do they tell you something about how you've been feeling or what you've been focused on during that time period? Journal about that.

3. **Cook something different.** Try cooking a type of food that you wouldn't normally eat, and cook it from scratch instead of using prepared seasoning mixes and jars. Or take a recipe you know and tweak it – add some other spices or something you wouldn't normally add. Notice how your taste buds react, and what the taste/smell of these foods evokes in your senses and memories – how they make you feel. Experiment – try a week of not eating meat, or a week of no dairy. Try eating one style of food for two or three days in a row, or designate a certain night of the week to some nation's dishes.

4. **Go on a scavenger walk.** Deliberately go for a walk with the aim of collecting stuff you see along the way. Another man's trash can be your treasure. Collect three or four things that interest you – a tin, a bolt, a piece of plastic, or even a leaf or a flower. See how you can use them in your creating or journaling.

5. **Go for a walk with your camera (or cell phone).** Take photos of things that catch your eye – maybe a flower, the shape of the clouds, a sign, the way a piece of rubbish is lying. Try different angles, close ups, filters. You can use the photos later in your journaling or collages, or you may even start

a new creative pastime. Going for a walk with your camera is also a great way to exercise, and is much more fun than "having to" exercise.

6. **Take a hike.** Get out into nature by yourself – to a park, the beach, or a forest. Let your thoughts wander as you walk and see where they end up (keep an eye on where you're going, though – don't get stranded at high tide or lost in the bush). Many ideas have come as people have gone walking. The writer Freidrich Nietzsche once said, "All truly great thoughts are conceived by walking." A 2014 Stanford study confirmed Nietzsche's suspicions – scientists Oppezzo and Schwartz revealed that walking boosts creativity by 60%.[17]

7. **Redecorate a room with things you already own.** When people think of redecorating, they may think of all the money that has to be spent to do so. But redecorating can be done simply, with stuff you already own. Decide what you want your redecorated room to look like, then go on a scavenger hunt around your house to find things suitable for that look. Dig into cupboards/storage boxes, check out your basement/attic/garage. Look at things you already own with new eyes – through the eyes of that design idea. Can a piece of furniture you already own be made suitable by using paint to change its look or by recovering it with fabric? Can an old grater become the base for a rustic kitchen clock? Can an old painter's drop cloth become new artsy cushions. Maybe you won't have to buy anything new at all to finish the room!

8. **Keep a dream journal.**[18] Many inventions and solutions

---

[17] http://blog.scribblepost.com/why-the-most-famous-people-in-history-took-long-walks/
http://news.stanford.edu/2014/04/24/walking-vs-sitting-042414/
[18] Great Books on Dream Interpretation: *Eyes to See* by Lyn Packer; *The Divinity Code* by Adrian Beale and Adam Thompson; *Dream Language* by James Goll; *Dream Encounters* by Barbie Breathitt.

MORE CREATIVITY ACTIVATORS

to problems have come to people in their dreams. Keep a dream journal beside your bed to write down your dreams when you wake up, so they aren't forgotten. Take notes of your dreams, writing down the broad theme and some of the details from them. There are some good books out there on dream interpretation, as well. Draw a picture of one of your dreams – our dreams are great indicators of what's going on in our daily lives. Draw what you saw in the dream and then ask yourself what the symbols mean to you – they might give you insight into things you are going through, or give you creative ideas.

9. **Listen to Music.** Make time to just sit and listen to music – whatever style you prefer, but especially classical. It can increase creativity and concentration, and it stimulates the part of the brain that controls motor actions.

10. **Make up a song.** You don't have to be a professional songwriter to write a song. The easiest way is to take a tune you know and put new words to it (you're not going to sell it, so you aren't breaking copyright laws at this stage). Make it happy, make it thoughtful, make it full of dreams or full of reality, make it anything you want – it's your song.

11. **Free write.**[19] The purpose of free writing is to get your creativity flowing, and to learn not to edit your words or thoughts as you write but to let them surface and flow. This exercise is great to do first thing in the morning; it clears your mind and kick-starts your creativity for the day. There are several ways to try free writing. All of them involve writing whatever comes into your mind over a set time frame, say 10 minutes, without stopping to read what you've written or

---
[19] Free writing – http://writingthroughlife.com/journal-writing-tips-the-benefits-of-free-writing/

judging what you're writing – no editing, censoring thoughts or correcting mistakes. This exercise helps you learn to write with flow, so that when you are writing other things you aren't always self-correcting as you write. One way to start your free writing is to use a prompt, like a subject, or a sentence from a story. Another is to start with whatever thought first comes into your mind, then continuing to write your thoughts from that starting place. Free writing is best done with pen and paper, not on a computer.

12. **Throw around some paint.** You may not be Jackson Pollack, but throwing paint at canvas can be incredibly stress releasing and fun. Obviously, make sure that you don't do it where you would ruin your carpet! Get a large cheap canvas and set it up somewhere in your backyard. Fill some squeeze bottles with paint (children's paint that is water soluble is great for this), or fill some water balloons with paint, and squeeze, throw, and see what happens. If you're a very structured person, this will stretch you hugely, as you'll have very little control over the outcome, but that is what makes it good for you. You may not produce a masterpiece, but that's not the object of the exercise. Take note of how you feel as you do this exercise; what buttons is it pushing and why? Or if you really can't bring yourself to do this on canvas, you could try it with watered-down children's paint or colored water on a sidewalk or driveway. Squirt away, make patterns, then hose it all away. This is a great activity to do with kids because you feel less self-conscious doing it.

13. **Learn a craft.** When we say the word "craft" we tend to think of something like knitting, but craftwork covers a wide variety of things – sewing, knitting, beadwork, welding,

woodworking, basket weaving, stained glass work, and more. Don't stereotype crafts, either; many men love knitting or needlework; women do welding and woodworking. There is such satisfaction in learning and mastering a craft and, what's more, you get the pleasure of seeing your creations give joy to people as they see or receive them. Your craftwork may even open up a whole new earning stream for you over time.

14. **Attend a night class.** Most colleges have night classes for people interested in learning new skills. They often cover a wide variety of topics, from computer work to cooking classes, photography, metal work, upholstery, spiritual pursuits and more. Check out your local college and see what they are offering; it's a great way to learn something new as well as to meet people you wouldn't normally associate with. Many people make new friends at night classes, and the friendships often carry on long after the class has finished.

15. **Use the last line.** Take the last line of a poem or paragraph and use it as the first line of something you write – turn it into a story, a song, a poem, an article, or journal entry.

16. **Reuse, refashion, repurpose.** Think of new uses for old objects – incorporate them into your creating. There are many ways that old things can be repurposed. "Vintage" and "retro" are in vogue as people again take note of the feelings of comfort and pride that "homemade" gives.

17. **Unleash your inner eccentric.** Do something that takes you out of your normal comfort zone, like – wearing mismatched socks, or arranging your desk space another way. Do something you wouldn't normally do. Go somewhere different for

lunch, eat something you wouldn't normally eat, dye your hair (it'll grow back; it's not forever). These things will jog you out of your normal habit patterns and get you out of your normal way of looking at things. This is always great for releasing creativity. For some great ideas to express your creativity in dress, look up "Advanced Style" in your Internet browser.

18. **Unleash your inner child.** Do something a child would do, something you haven't done for years – finger-paint, play on the swings at the local park, or build a wooden block tower. Have a picnic with your teddy bears, under the dining table (yes, I have done this one). Play with your kids' (or grandkids') Legos (just don't leave them on the floor for someone to step on). Take note of how you feel. Journal about the experience. Have fun; sometimes adulthood gets far too serious. Life was always meant to be an adventure, not just a series of problems to be solved.

19. **Do a day of silence.** We live in a world besieged by sound. Allow yourself time to be silent – to listen to your thoughts, your heart, your inner voice, God. Go someplace where you can draw aside and not have to interact with people – a retreat center, a motel, or a local monastery or convent (they sometimes have day rooms where people can come and be silent). Turn off your devices or, better still, leave them at home so they won't tempt you to turn them on.

20. **Choose a day from your childhood.** Remember how you felt on that day – the sights, smells, weather, etc. Take one of those things ("it was a rainy day…"), tap into the emotion of it, and create something or journal it. Do you have any photos of that day? If so, use one of them in your entry.

MORE CREATIVITY ACTIVATORS

21. **Right now I feel…** How do you feel right now? Use it as a starter. Allow yourself to explore the emotion, and write, using expressive, feeling words as you write. Use color, form and even texture to portray the feeling. Don't just do it superficially, but drill down into those feeling words until you get to the real reason behind the feeling. Feeling "blah" might in fact be, "I am worried about the test coming up," or something similar. Feeling happy might drill down to, "I'm proud of myself; I gave that my best shot." Drilling down allows you to get to the bottom of a feeling, understand it, and do something about it.

22. **Start a blog.** Get your thoughts and creativity out there into the world. Write, use photos, recipes, or whatever you want – it's your blog! If you do choose to start a blog and you don't like it, you can stop. You may choose to continue it or not; stopping does not make you a failure, it simply means that you decided it wasn't a high priority for you, and that's okay.

23. **Do some inspirational posts to Facebook or Instagram.** I post regular prophetic encouragements on a Facebook page.[20] Those prophetic encouragements have blessed thousands over the time I've been doing them. If you want to try something like this, there are many free apps and programs you can use.[21]

24. **Use a quote** – Why do you like that quote? What does it inspire in you? How does it make you feel? Words evoke images. What images does it bring to mind? What color do you think of when you read it? What does it suggest, what

---

[20] Type the following into your search engine or Facebook finder space and it will show my Facebook page – @creativepropheticcommunicator

[21] To create pictures for the posts, I use a free app called Word Swag, and Photoshop. You can also use Canva, plus many other available programs and apps.

story does it have to tell you? Use the quote as the prompt for doing something creative.

25. **Make your mark in public.** Have you tried graffiti, yarn-bombing, stencil art, moss art, 3-D chalk drawings, Lego graffiti in sidewalk cracks and on buildings, and much more? (Check Google for cool pictures.) Urban art is huge – it's not just graffiti – there are many different expressions. Beautify your surroundings! A simple way to start is to: 1) Make erasable graffiti: Practice a simple line drawing. Taking some chalk with you (in a small plastic bag so your pocket doesn't get dirty), draw on the footpath. You could draw a crazy hopscotch. I guarantee that people will try the hopscotch. The rain will wash it away, but before it does people will smile when they see it, and they will try it out! 2) Draw a picture, photocopy/print a dozen copies, and tape them to random lamp posts for people to view as they walk by. It can be as simple as a large daisy (just make sure you aren't breaking any of your city laws or ordinances).

26. **Make some give-away art.** One lady makes small cloth dolls and leaves them in public places (park benches, bus stops or on buses). She puts them in plastic bags with a note: "This is a free gift. Take it and keep it or pass it on." She includes an email address so people can tell her the story of the doll's journey. Another idea is that maybe you could do some stone art. Draw patterns or inspirational quotes on stones with a sharpie, or use paint. Leave them somewhere for people to find as a blessing.

27. **Write your emotions a letter.** Begin with, "Dear __ (sadness, joy, boredom, happiness, anger, etc.), and sign it as you would normally. Be honest with how you feel about the

MORE CREATIVITY ACTIVATORS

emotion: what you like about it, what you want to change, and how you want to change it, etc.

28. **Practice everyday appreciation.** Take note of the people around you. What do you appreciate about them? Write a note or card and tell them – celebrate them!

29. **Do brain puzzles or crosswords.** Brain puzzles and crosswords boost your problem solving skills – in others words, they make you more creative. They are also good for keeping your brain active and young. You can buy books full of them, or find them online at a huge number of sites.

30. **Cultivate wonder.** Wonder is something that we can lose as we become more 'adult' and supposedly more 'sophisticated', yet that's not necessarily a good thing. Lose wonder and life will become mundane and jaded, and you'll soon lose appreciation and thankfulness, too. Find something ordinary like a flower and really think about it; appreciate its beauty, form, complexity, and fragrance, and also appreciate its Creator, too. Give yourself permission to feel the wonder. Be in the moment, allow the emotion of it to register, and cultivate it.

31. **Turn the TV off.** TV can be a creativity thief if we let it; set a goal – one week, two weeks, or a month with no TV, and watch your creativity and your relationships blossom. Take the time to do things you wouldn't normally do; learn a craft, go to a night class, have a game night with friends, read a book, paint a room in your house, talk with your spouse, etc. There is no end to the things you can do with the extra time you'll have.

All around you, every day, there are chances for you to explore new things or put your creativity to work – in solving problems, creating solutions, helping someone else, or simply to beautify your world. I often find myself caught up with wonder over the amount and variety of the creativity I see around me daily. That book cover in the bookstore, that invention, the ironwork on a fence, the things I see online, the books I read – all these things inspire me and encourage me to keep pushing my boundaries, to try new creative endeavors. I hope you will keep pushing your boundaries, too. Who knows, you might just imagine, and then create, something that will leave the world a far richer place because you used the creativity you were born with!

Extra Features

Bonus Chapter

The Value of Your Values

Your values are as individual to you as fingerprints and, like fingerprints, your values leave their imprint on everything you do.

Values – you may think that's a funny thing to be talking about in a book on creativity, but in creativity, as in any other area of life, values will play a key role. They are the fundamental beliefs and principles that a person lives from, and they dictate our behaviour and actions; yet, many people never consciously think about them. At first glance you may be tempted to think that creativity and values are strange companions.

Most of us have a mixture of both positive and negative values that we live from, consciously or unconsciously. Many things dictate and form what our values are, such as our early childhood experiences, family culture, national culture, schools and institutions, and religious background. Some examples of positive values are honesty, honoring people, and kindness, while negative values may be things like dishonesty, isolation, stinginess, manipulation, disloyalty, suspicion, etc. Negative values are usually formed in our lives when positive values are either not represented or are violated repeatedly.

As Mahatma Ghandi said, "Your beliefs become your thoughts. Your thoughts become your words. Your words become your actions. Your actions become your habits. Your habits become your values. Your values become your destiny."

Values can, and do, change during our lifetime, depending on life circumstances and how we react to them over a period of time. Habitual reactions can set up new values in our lives. And in certain seasons of life we give more weight, and operate more strongly, out of particular values.

Your values form part of who you are. They help make up your identity and character, and they are key to all that you do – you'll either live up to who you know you are, or betray who you know you are. Identify the values that you live from, keep the positive beliefs, and change the negative beliefs and actions that have come from values being violated. Negative beliefs can be changed.

"You will know the truth, and the truth will set you free."
—*John 8:32*

Knowing the truth is the doorway to freedom. You may have to deal with soul wounds, be persistent in believing that truth, intentionally focus on renewing your mind, and change your behavior, but it will be worth it. It is not enough to just acknowledge the truth; you need to realize that truth is experiential as well as intellectual. Truth is, in fact, contained in the person of Jesus, and it's by experiencing the reality of His love for you, His good intentions toward you, and His plans to bless you, that you will be established in the truth.

Know Your Values

One way you can find your core internal values is by asking yourself, "What things make me really angry?" If injustice makes you really angry then, quite possibly, justice is one of your core internal values. If you hate being like everyone else, then individuality may be a core value. If you dislike people being dishonored and not recognized, then honor may be a core value.

Values are the foundation blocks that you build your life on, and they can be used as a guide in any situation – "How does this situation stack up against my values?" If it falls short, or overrides your core values, then seriously think about whether you should do it or not. Knowing what your values are also makes life decisions easier. Their importance and usefulness in daily life cannot be overestimated.

Sometimes your friends can tell you the values you live by better than you can. That's what happened to me. One day a friend and I were talking about values, and she said, "Oh, I can tell you two of your values straight away," and she mentioned enjoyment and individuality. I would never have recognized that without her saying it, but when she did, I realized that she was right; those two values play a huge part in how I live. If something is not enjoyable to me I have to make it enjoyable somehow, or else make a deliberate choice to do it despite how I feel.

The following is a list of commonly acknowledged values used by counselors and leadership around the world to help people understand how they respond to their world. I have listed beside some of them the negative value that happens when the positive value is repeatedly violated.

- Achievement / Inaction
- Adventure
- Authenticity / Inauthenticity
- Authority
- Autonomy
- Balance / Imbalance, Workaholic
- Beauty
- Boldness
- Challenge
- Citizenship
- Community / Isolationism
- Compassion / Intolerance
- Competency
- Connectivity / Distance
- Contribution
- Creativity / Non-creative
- Curiosity
- Determination / Indecision
- Devotion
- Enjoyment
- Exploration
- Fairness

- Faith
- Fame
- Family
- Friendships / Aloneness
- Fun / Seriousness
- Growth
- Happiness
- Honesty /Dishonesty
- Honour / Dishonour
- Humour
- Individuality / Conformity
- Influence
- Inner Harmony / Dis-ease
- Intimacy / Unfriendliness
- Justice
- Kindness / Inconsideration
- Knowledge / Ignorance
- Leadership
- Learning
- Love / Ambivalence, Worthlessness
- Loyalty
- Making a Difference

- Meaningful Work
- Openness / Protectiveness
- Optimism
- Peace
- Pleasure
- Poise
- Popularity
- Prosperity / Poverty Spirit
- Recognition
- Religion / Independence
- Reputation
- Respect
- Responsibility / Entitlement
- Security
- Self-Respect / Self-hatred
- Service
- Spirituality
- Stability
- Status
- Success / Failure
- Trustworthiness
- Wealth / Wasteful, Hoarding
- Wisdom

Values and the Creative Process

Values have a definite relationship to our creativity because the values we live from affect how we approach everything. In creativity, if you deny who you are and try to be a copy of someone else, you'll just end up being frustrated. It's okay to admire and learn from other people's style, but you are not them; you have to be yourself and express your creativity in a way that is authentically you. For example, I love realism in art and I admire people who can make a painting of a subject look as though the real thing is in front of you. But I can't do realism in my work. I always want to add stuff, change it around, abstract it a bit, and that's okay, that's my style. If I tried to squeeze myself into the photographic realism style, I would end up frustrated and, eventually, possibly, even doubt my creative abilities.

Knowing your values also helps you in other ways. For example, if respect for life is a strong value, then you're probably not going to do art works that promote anarchy and social decay. If honoring and valuing people is something you strongly believe in, then you probably won't use images that demean people in your advertising campaigns. It becomes an easy decision – "That's not who I am." If we don't know our values, then when we do something that unknowingly contravenes one of our internal values we will feel uneasy about what we've done, and it will never sit quite right with us. It might be a brilliant bit of creativity and technical excellence, but we will never fully feel at peace about it.

When working with others on projects, we can sometimes be tempted to compromise our values. If you are in the workplace and are part of a team, there will inevitably be things that others do that will annoy you. If harmony is one of your internal values, then the team being able to function in harmony becomes important to you. If honoring other people is one of your values, then you will be careful what you say to them – you'll be honest, but you will speak and act toward them lovingly.

The effects of betraying a core value

When a person compromises their values, it has an effect. They end up feeling guilty, and they know in their heart that they've not been true to themselves. That colors the way they see themselves, others, and the project they're working on. When people compromise their values, they instinctively withdraw to some degree or another from the project, or from those involved in it. This can also lead to a feeling of letting themselves and possibly others down, which then causes feelings of guilt and self-reproach. If a person compromises their values on a consistent basis, they'll end up cementing negative thoughts and feelings about themselves into their lives, which may then have effects on their health and well being.

If we find that we are consistently compromising on our values in situations, then we must look at how we view ourselves and our contribution. We must learn to value and honor ourselves rightly if we want the creativity within us to be released to its fullest.

Sometimes we may feel guilty yet not have done anything we can recognize as being "wrong." In those times, check to see if perhaps one of your core values has been violated. That violation of values can happen through others, or through our own actions. When that happens we need to ask ourselves why we are feeling this, and work through it.

THE VALUE OF YOUR VALUES

 ## Creativity Activator 1

- Look over the list of values contained in this chapter and make a list of some of your values – those internal things that you live by, the things that are important to you and will be your non-negotiable values.

- Choose the five that you resonate most strongly with. These will most likely be some of the base values that you live from. Be honest. Don't choose the expected Christian response – we all know that love should be a foundational value in our lives, but if we were never shown love it may not truly be one yet. There is no shame in that; it simply shows you an area that the Father will want to heal and restore in your life.

 ## Creativity Activator 2

- In this activation you'll make a collage of your values – you'll need a large sheet of paper to do it on. This collage will show your values in visual form – things like honesty, truth, love, fun, friendship, communication, uniqueness, etc. Find pictures that relate to those values from old magazines or on the Internet; cut out words, write out quotes or find songs that have those values in. Arrange them artfully and stick them on the paper, using pens or colored pencils to further enhance the collage. Pin up your collage where you can see it often. It will inspire you and remind you that these are valuable to you!

Scripture References on Creativity and Imagination

All life is a reflection of the wondrous creativity of God.

This collection of Scripture verses on different aspects of creativity and imagination is not exhaustive. These are just some of the ones that I have found over the years as I've looked at these subjects. I've tried to include references to every type of creativity mentioned in Scripture, but I haven't included all of the references that there are. For example, singing and music have far more references than are mentioned here.

Where the original meaning of certain words used in the Scriptures is unclear, I have placed the words and their meaning at the end of the Scripture reference in brackets.

Creativity - God's and ours

In the beginning God created the heavens and the earth.
—Genesis 1:1

God created the great sea monsters and every living creature that moves, with which the waters swarmed after their kind, and every winged bird after its kind; and God saw that it was good." —*Genesis 1:21*

Then God said, "Let us make mankind in our image, in our likeness, so that they may rule over the fish in the sea and the birds in the sky, over the livestock and all the wild animals, and over all the creatures that move along the ground." So God created mankind in his own image, in the image of God he created them; male and female he created them. God blessed them and said to them, "Be fruitful and increase in number; fill the earth and subdue it. Rule over the fish in the sea and the birds in the sky and over every living creature that moves on the ground." Then God said, "I give you every seed-bearing plant on the face of the whole earth and every tree that has fruit with seed in it. They will be yours for food. And to all the beasts of the earth and all the birds in the sky and all the creatures that move along the ground—everything that has the breath of life in it—I give every green plant for food." And it was so. —*Genesis 1:26-30 NIV*

God saw all that he had made, and it was very good. And there was evening, and there was morning—the sixth day.
—*Genesis 1:31 NIV*

Then God blessed the seventh day and made it holy, because on it he rested from all the work of creating that he had done. —*Genesis 2:3 NIV*

This is the account of the heavens and the earth when they were created, when the Lord God made the earth and the heavens. —*Genesis 2:4 NIV*

SCRIPTURE REFERENCES ON CREATIVITY AND IMAGINATION

Then the Lord God formed the man of dust from the ground and breathed into his nostrils the breath of life, and the man became a living creature." —*Genesis 2:7 ESV*

Then the Lord God said, "It is not good that the man should be alone; I will make him a helper fit for him."
—*Genesis 2:18 ESV*

His brother's name was Jubal; he was the father of all those who play the lyre and pipe. —*Genesis 4:21*

"You shall not make for yourself a carved image, or any likeness of anything that is in heaven above, or that is in the earth beneath, or that is in the water under the earth."
—*Exodus 20:4 ESV*

The Lord said to Moses, "Speak to the people of Israel, that they take for me a contribution. From every man whose heart moves him you shall receive the contribution for me. And this is the contribution that you shall receive from them: gold, silver, and bronze, blue and purple and scarlet yarns and fine twined linen, goats' hair, tanned rams' skins, goatskins, acacia wood." —*Exodus 25:1-5 ESV*

"And see that you make them after the pattern for them, which is being shown you on the mountain."
—*Exodus 25:40 ESV*

"Moreover, you shall make the tabernacle with ten curtains of fine twined linen and blue and purple and scarlet yarns; you shall make them with cherubim skillfully worked into them. The length of each curtain shall be twenty-eight cubits, and the breadth of each curtain four cubits; all the curtains shall be the same size. Five curtains shall be coupled to one

another, and the other five curtains shall be coupled to one another. And you shall make loops of blue on the edge of the outermost curtain in the first set. Likewise you shall make loops on the edge of the outermost curtain in the second set. Fifty loops you shall make on the one curtain, and fifty loops you shall make on the edge of the curtain that is in the second set; the loops shall be opposite one another."
—Exodus 26:1-5 ESV

"…and he has filled him with the Spirit of God, with skill, with intelligence, with knowledge, and with all craftsmanship, to devise artistic designs, to work in gold and silver and bronze." *—Exodus 35:31-32 ESV*

"He has filled them with skill to do every sort of work done by an engraver or by a designer or by an embroiderer in blue and purple and scarlet yarns and fine twined linen, or by a weaver—by any sort of workman or skilled designer."
—Exodus 35:35 ESV

And all the craftsmen among the workmen made the tabernacle with ten curtains. They were made of fine twined linen and blue and purple and scarlet yarns, with cherubim skillfully worked. *—Exodus 36:8 ESV*

"'Cursed be the man who makes a carved or cast metal image, an abomination to the LORD, a thing made by the hands of a craftsman, and sets it up in secret.' And all the people shall answer and say, 'Amen.'" *—Deuteronomy 27:15 ESV*

"Behold, I give you a wise and discerning mind, so that none like you has been before you and none like you shall arise after you." *—1 Kings 3:12 ESV*

SCRIPTURE REFERENCES ON CREATIVITY AND IMAGINATION

And God gave Solomon wisdom and understanding beyond measure, and breadth of mind like the sand on the seashore, so that Solomon's wisdom surpassed the wisdom of all the people of the east and all the wisdom of Egypt. For he was wiser than all other men, wiser than Ethan the Ezrahite, and Heman, Calcol, and Darda, the sons of Mahol, and his fame was in all the surrounding nations. He also spoke 3,000 proverbs, and his songs were 1,005. —*1 Kings 4:29-32 ESV*

"You have an abundance of workmen: stonecutters, masons, carpenters, and all kinds of craftsmen without number, skilled in working gold, silver, bronze, and iron. Arise and work! The LORD be with you!" —*1 Chronicles 22:15 ESV*

David also commanded the chiefs of the Levites to appoint their brothers as the singers who should play loudly on musical instruments, on harps and lyres and cymbals, to raise sounds of joy. —*1 Chronicles 15:16 ESV*

"The house that I am to build will be great, for our God is greater than all gods. But who is able to build him a house, since heaven, even highest heaven, cannot contain him? Who am I to build a house for him, except as a place to make offerings before him? So now send me a man skilled to work in gold, silver, bronze, and iron, and in purple, crimson, and blue fabrics, trained also in engraving, to be with the skilled workers who are with me in Judah and Jerusalem, whom David my father provided." —*2 Chronicles 2:5-7 ESV*

"…the son of a woman of the daughters of Dan, and his father was a man of Tyre. He is trained to work in gold, silver, bronze, iron, stone, and wood, and in purple, blue, and crimson fabrics and fine linen, and to do all sorts of engraving

and execute any design that may be assigned him, with your craftsmen, the craftsmen of my lord, David your father."
—*2 Chronicles 2:14 ESV*

"Oh that my words were written! Oh that they were inscribed in a book! Oh that with an iron pen and lead they were engraved in the rock forever!" —*Job 19:23-24 ESV*

"But it is the spirit in man, the breath of the Almighty, that makes him understand." —*Job 32:8 ESV*

O Lord, our Lord, how majestic is your name in all the earth! You have set your glory above the heavens. Out of the mouth of babies and infants, you have established strength because of your foes, to still the enemy and the avenger. When I look at your heavens, the work of your fingers, the moon and the stars, which you have set in place, what is man that you are mindful of him, and the son of man that you care for him? Yet you have made him a little lower than the heavenly beings and crowned him with glory and honor. —*Psalm 8:1-5 ESV*

The heavens declare the glory of God, and the sky above proclaims his handiwork. —*Psalm 19:1 ESV*

By the word of the Lord the heavens were made, and by the breath of his mouth all their host. —*Psalm 33:6 ESV*

My heart overflows with a pleasing theme; I address my verses to the king; my tongue is like the pen of a ready scribe.
—*Psalm 45:1 ESV*

Oh sing to the Lord a new song; sing to the Lord, all the earth! —*Psalm 96:1 ESV*

SCRIPTURE REFERENCES ON CREATIVITY AND IMAGINATION

O Lord, how manifold are your works! In wisdom have you made them all; the earth is full of your creatures.
—*Psalm 104:24 ESV*

Our help is in the name of the Lord, who made heaven and earth. —*Psalm 124:8 ESV*

I praise you, for I am fearfully and wonderfully made. Wonderful are your works; my soul knows it very well.
—*Psalm 139:14 ESV*

Let them praise the name of the Lord! For he commanded and they were created. —*Psalms 148:5 ESV*

Praise the Lord! Sing to the Lord a new song, and His praise in the congregation of the godly ones. —*Psalm 149:1*

Praise the Lord! Praise God in his sanctuary; praise him in his mighty heavens! Praise him for his mighty deeds; praise him according to his excellent greatness! Praise him with trumpet sound; praise him with lute and harp! Praise him with tambourine and dance; praise him with strings and pipe! Praise him with sounding cymbals; praise him with loud clashing cymbals! Let everything that has breath praise the Lord! Praise the Lord! —*Psalm 150:1-6 ESV*

Do you see a man skillful in his work? He will stand before kings; he will not stand before obscure men.
—*Proverbs 22:29 ESV*

It is the glory of God to conceal things, but the glory of kings is to search things out. —*Proverbs 25:2 ESV*

She opens her hand to the poor and reaches out her hands to the needy. She is not afraid of snow for her household, for all her household are clothed in scarlet. She makes bed coverings for herself; her clothing is fine linen and purple. Her husband is known in the gates when he sits among the elders of the land. She makes linen garments and sells them; she delivers sashes to the merchant. —*Proverbs 31:20-24 ESV*

He has made everything beautiful in its time.
—*Ecclesiastes 3:11 ESV*

Lift up your eyes on high and see who has created these stars, The One who leads forth their host by number, He calls them all by name; because of the greatness of His might and the strength of His power, not one of them is missing."
—*Isaiah 40:26*

Do you not know? Have you not heard? The Lord is the everlasting God, the Creator of the ends of the earth. He will not grow tired or weary, and his understanding no one can fathom. —*Isaiah 40:28 NIV*

…that they may see and know, may consider and understand together, that the hand of the Lord has done this, the Holy One of Israel has created it. —*Isaiah 41:20 ESV*

Thus says God, the Lord, who created the heavens and stretched them out, who spread out the earth and what comes from it, who gives breath to the people on it and spirit to those who walk in it: —*Isaiah 42:5 ESV*

Even every one that is called by my name: for I have created him for my glory, I have formed him; yea, I have made him.
—*Isaiah 43:7 KJV*

"Woe to him who strives with him who formed him, a pot among earthen pots! Does the clay say to him who forms it, 'What are you making?' or 'Your work has no handles?'"
—Isaiah 45:9 ESV

For this is what the Lord says—he who created the heavens, he is God; he who fashioned and made the earth, he founded it; he did not create it to be empty, but formed it to be inhabited—he says: "I am the Lord, and there is no other."
—Isaiah 45:18 NIV

"For you shall go out in joy and be led forth in peace; the mountains and the hills before you shall break forth into singing, and all the trees of the field shall clap their hands."
—Isaiah 55:12 ESV

But now, O Lord, you are our Father; we are the clay, and you are our potter; we are all the work of your hand.
—Isaiah 64:8 ESV

For, behold, I create new heavens and a new earth: and the former shall not be remembered, nor come into mind.
—Isaiah 65:17 KJV

Whatever your hand finds to do, do it with your might.
—Ecclesiastes 9:10 ESV

It is he who made the earth by his power, who established the world by his wisdom, and by his understanding stretched out the heavens.
—Jeremiah 10:12 ESV

So I went down to the potter's house, and there he was working at his wheel.
—Jeremiah 18:3 ESV

"'Ah, Lord God! It is you who have made the heavens and the earth by your great power and by your outstretched arm! Nothing is too hard for you.'" —*Jeremiah 32:17 ESV*

For Ezra had set his heart to study the law of the Lord and to practice [it] and to teach [His] statutes and ordinances in Israel … to Ezra the priest, the scribe of the law of the God of heaven. —*Ezra 7:10-12*

As for these four youths, God gave them learning and skill in all literature and wisdom, and Daniel had understanding in all visions and dreams. —*Daniel 1:17 ESV*

I have also spoken to [you by] the prophets, and I have multiplied visions [for you] and [have appealed to you] through parables acted out by the prophets. —*Hosea 12:10 AMPC*

For behold, he who forms the mountains and creates the wind, and declares to man what is his thought, who makes the morning darkness, and treads on the heights of the earth—the Lord, the God of hosts, is his name!"
—*Amos 4:13 ESV*

And the Lord answered me: "Write the vision; make it plain on tablets, so he may run who reads it."
—*Habakkuk 2:2 ESV*

"The Lord your God is with you, the Mighty Warrior who saves. He will take great delight in you; in his love he will no longer rebuke you, but will rejoice over you with singing."
—*Zephaniah 3:17 NIV*

"Therefore every scribe who has been trained for the kingdom of heaven is like a master of a house, who brings out of his treasure what is new and what is old." [scribe: writer, teacher, interpreter of sacred writings] —*Matthew 13:52 ESV*

"He who had received the five talents went at once and traded with them, and he made five talents more."
—*Matthew 25:16 ESV*

"For life is more than food, and the body more than clothing." —*Luke 12:23 ESV*

All things were made through him, and without him was not any thing made that was made. —*John 1:3 ESV*

For the invisible things of him from the creation of the world are clearly seen, being understood by the things that are made, even his eternal power and Godhead; so that they are without excuse. —*Romans 1:20 KJV*

For the gifts and the calling of God are irrevocable.
—*Romans 11:29 ESV*

Having gifts that differ according to the grace given to us, let us use them: if prophecy, in proportion to our faith.
—*Romans 12:6 ESV*

According to the grace of God given to me, like a skilled master builder I laid a foundation, and someone else is building upon it. Let each one take care how he builds upon it.
—*1 Corinthians 3:10 ESV*

Let all that you do be done in love.
—*1 Corinthians 16:14 ESV*

Therefore if any man be in Christ, he is a new creature: old things are passed away; behold, all things are become new.
—*2 Corinthians 5:17 KJV*

For we are his workmanship, created in Christ Jesus unto good works, which God hath before ordained that we should walk in them. —*Ephesians 2:10 KJV*

...and to make plain to everyone the administration of this mystery, which for ages past was kept hidden in God, who created all things. —*Ephesians 3:9 NIV*

Now to him who is able to do far more abundantly than all that we ask or think, according to the power at work within us... —*Ephesians 3:20 ESV*

...be filled with the Spirit, addressing one another in psalms and hymns and spiritual songs, singing and making melody to the Lord with your heart. —*Ephesians 5:18-19 ESV*

Have this mind among yourselves, which is yours in Christ Jesus. —*Philippians 2:5 ESV*

He is the image of the invisible God, the firstborn of all creation. —*Colossians 1:15 ESV*

For by him were all things created, that are in heaven, and that are in earth, visible and invisible, whether they be thrones, or dominions, or principalities, or powers: all things were created by him, and for him. —*Colossians 1:16 KJV*

Let the word of Christ dwell in you richly in all wisdom; teaching and admonishing one another in psalms and hymns

SCRIPTURE REFERENCES ON CREATIVITY AND IMAGINATION

and spiritual songs, singing with grace in your hearts to the Lord. —*Colossians 3:16 KJV*

Whatever you do, work heartily, as for the Lord and not for men... —*Colossians 3:23 ESV*

For everything created by God is good, and nothing is to be rejected if it is received with thanksgiving...
—*1 Timothy 4:4 ESV*

Do not neglect the gift you have, which was given you by prophecy when the council of elders laid their hands on you. Practice these things, immerse yourself in them, so that all may see your progress. —*1 Timothy 4:14-15 ESV*

All scripture is given by inspiration of God, and is profitable for doctrine, for reproof, for correction, for instruction in righteousness. —*2 Timothy 3:16 KJV*

"But in these last days he has spoken to us by his Son, whom he appointed the heir of all things, through whom also he created the world." —*Hebrews 1:2 ESV*

(For every house is built by someone, but the builder of all things is God.) —*Hebrews 3:4 ESV*

By faith we understand that the universe was created by the word of God, so that what is seen was not made out of things that are visible. —*Hebrews 11:3 ESV*

"Worthy are You, our Lord and our God, to receive glory and honor and power; for You created all things, and because of Your will they existed, and were created." —*Revelation 4:11*

Imagination

And God saw that the wickedness of man was great in the earth, and that every imagination of the thoughts of his heart was only evil continually. —*Genesis 6:5 KJV*

Behold, the people is one, and they have all one language; and this they begin to do: and now nothing will be restrained from them, which they have imagined to do.
—*Genesis 11:6 KJV*

This book of the law shall not depart from your mouth, but you shall meditate on it day and night ... then you will make your way prosperous, and then you will have success." [meditate = imagine, ponder] —*Joshua 1:8*

Above all else, guard your heart, for everything you do flows from it. [heart = mind, heart, imagination]
—*Proverbs 4:23 NIV*

Roll your works upon the Lord, [commit and trust them wholly to Him; He will cause your thoughts to become agreeable to His will, and] so shall your plans be established and succeed. [thoughts = intentions, inventions, imaginations, calculations] —*Proverbs 16:3 AMPC*

But they hearkened not, nor inclined their ear, but walked in the counsels and in the imagination of their evil heart, and went backward, and not forward. —*Jeremiah 7:24 KJV*

But have walked after the imagination of their own heart, and after Baalim, which their fathers taught them.
—*Jeremiah 9:14 KJV*

SCRIPTURE REFERENCES ON CREATIVITY AND IMAGINATION

...everyone who looks at a woman with lust for her has already committed adultery with her in his heart. —*Matthew 5:28*

You shall love the Lord your God with all your heart, and with all your soul, and with all your mind. [imagination]
—*Matthew 22:37*

He has shown strength with his arm; he has scattered the proud in the thoughts of their hearts. —*Luke 1:51 ESV*

And seek not ye what ye shall eat, or what ye shall drink, neither be ye of doubtful mind. [mind = imagination]
—*Luke 12:29 KJV*

For even though they knew God, they did not honor Him as God or give thanks, but they became futile in their speculations, and their foolish heart was darkened.. [speculations = imaginings, thoughts] —*Romans 1:21*

God ... calls those things which are not as though they were. —*Romans 4:17 King James 2000*

...while we look not at the things which are seen, but at the things which are not seen... [seen – the visible; unseen – the invisible, intangible) —*2 Corinthians 4:18*

...casting down arguments and every high thing that exalts itself against the knowledge of God, bringing every thought into captivity to the obedience of Christ.
—*2 Corinthians 10:5 NKJV*

God ... may give unto you the spirit of wisdom and revelation ... that the eyes of your understanding being enlightened: That ye may know what is the hope of his calling,... [understanding = deep thought, imagination] —*Ephesians 1:17-18 KJV*

So this I say, and affirm together with the Lord, that you walk no longer just as the Gentiles also walk, in the futility of their mind, being darkened in their understanding, excluded from the life of God ... But you did not learn Christ in this way ... Put on the new self, which in the likeness of God has been created in righteousness and holiness of the truth. [mind = logical reasoning mind; understanding = imagination]
—*Ephesians 4:17-18,20,24*

And you, that were once alienated and enemies in your mind by wicked works, yet now has he reconciled... [mind = imagination]   —*Colossians 1:21 King James 2000*

Let no man despise thy youth;... give attendance to reading, to exhortation, to doctrine. Neglect not the gift that is in thee, which was given thee by prophecy, with the laying on of the hands ... Meditate upon these things; give thyself wholly to them; that thy profiting may appear to all. [meditate = imagine, revolve in the mind]   —*1 Timothy 4:12-15 KJV*

By faith he left Egypt, not being afraid of the anger of the king, for he endured as seeing him who is invisible. [seeing = to stare at, to discern clearly either physically or mentally. Moses saw him face-to-face physically and mentally]
—*Hebrews 11:27 ESV*

And we know that the Son of God has come and has given us understanding, so that we may know him who is true; and we are in him who is true, in his son Jesus Christ. He is the true God and eternal life. [understanding = imagination]
—*1 John 5:20 ESV*

Study Guide Questions

Questions and curiosity are both vitally important in developing creativity. Without a questioning mind, life would become stagnant and the status quo would reign.

The questions below are only a guide; you may stick to them or come up with better ones as you create some of your own. You may get through all of them, or only one or two in a meeting. The goal isn't to get through them all but to encourage open and honest discussion about creativity and its place in our lives.

At the end of each discussion time, take a few minutes to make sure that everyone is okay. Some people will share things that have had a deep effect on their lives. I encourage you to spend some time at the end of each session and pray with one another concerning the things that came up during the discussion. Encourage each other to believe God that creativity will blossom and develop into something that blesses them individually, as well as blessing others. Also encourage people to try to do something creative during the coming week to bless someone else.

Introductory Meeting

- Talk about the aims for the group; spend some time looking at the chapter on how to use the book individually and as a group. As a group, discuss and set any group expectations or guidelines for involvement. Write them out and make sure everyone is in agreement with them; that way, as you go forward you can hold each other accountable to the group agreement when you need to.

- Ask each person to share what they hope to get out of the study, what expectations they have, and any reservations that they may have. Pair the people up and have them pray for each other about the things they've just shared.

- Set homework for week one: Read the chapter, "What's So Important About Creativity?" and do the personal activations contained in that chapter.

"What's So Important About Creativity?"

- Discuss the idea that we are all born creative. Was that concept new to anyone? What does realizing that mean to you?

- Explore the idea people have that some are creative and some aren't. What makes people think that?

- Discuss the ways this chapter challenged your thinking on how creative you are in everyday life.

- How did it change the way you approach your daily life?

- In what ways did you recognize your creativity at work in the everyday things you do?

STUDY GUIDE QUESTIONS

- Discuss the idea of co-creating your life with God. What does that mean, and what does it look like in action?
- How much autonomy or freedom do you feel you have to make decisions?
- How much have you actively dreamed and created the type of life God says we can have?
- In what ways are you living an actively curious life?
- Set next week's homework: Read the chapter, "God and Creativity," and do the personal activations.

God and Creativity

- What do the two verses mentioned at the beginning of the chapter tell us about God's creativity?
- As you reviewed the Scriptures about creativity at the back of the book – which ones surprised you, and why?
- What does it mean for us to be made in God's image as a creative being?
- What restrictions does God place around our creativity, and does He actively encourage it or discourage it in any way?
- What restrictions should we place around our creativity as a result of that?
- What are some ways that we could use creativity in our worship times as individuals or as church communities?
- Set next week's homework: Read the chapter, "Imagine That," and do the personal activations.

Imagine That!

- Discuss the most common views on imagination – good, wicked, used only for fantasizing and making things up, an escape from life, useful in creativity, not important, not worth bothering over, only for creative people.

- As a group, talk about any of the verses that gave you insight into how God views our imagination. What was it that impacted you about those verses? Why?

- Discuss the concept that the eyes of our heart/mind/understanding can see the invisible realms. What does that mean for your life?

- Discuss how imagination and fear work together in your life, and what you can do to bring your fears under control?

- Discuss how negative words spoken by ourselves, or others, can affect our imagination – even to the point of shutting it down.

- Set next week's homework: Read the chapter, "Losing Me, Finding Me," and do the personal activations.

Losing Me, Finding Me

- Discuss some of the ways that we either encourage or squash creativity. What can we do to focus more on encouragement?

- What part has creativity had in our lives as kids, in education, as adults, in our jobs?

- How does our life suffer when we aren't using our creativity? Share personal stories.

STUDY GUIDE QUESTIONS

- How can we promote and foster creativity in our homes, in our churches, and in our schools and communities?
- Talk about the effects that creativity killers have on us. Have people in the group recognized them at work in their lives?
- Set next week's homework: Read the chapter, "Oh, the Possibilities!" and do the personal activations.

Oh, the Possibilities!

- Discuss the mindsets that people have about creativity and why we have those mindsets. What can be done to break out of any negative ones?
- How does stereotyping play a role in different expressions of creativity and in our willingness to try them?
- Talk about the effects of repressing your creativity. Have you had any of them happen in your personal life experience? If so, how did it affect you?
- Talk about how the group has viewed ideas of success and failure, and if that has changed after reading this chapter.
- If you have time, share with each other what creative expressions or endeavors you would like to try in the coming year.
- Set next week's homework: Read the chapter, "The Creative Process," and do the personal activations.

The Creative Process

- Think about times when you've been creating something or working on a project. As you look back on them, in what ways did you recognize the creative process happening?

- If you are working on a project currently, what part of the creative process are you going through?

- Are there parts of the creative process where you often "hit the wall"? Why do you think that is? What thoughts are limiting you?

- Discuss how often your emotions get in the way of the process flow while you are creating.

- Discuss the "inevitable problem" and ways you can future-proof against those problems sidetracking you or causing you to put off your project. For example, are there affirmations that you can post on your mirror or noticeboard? Are there people you can talk to, who will encourage you through this rough patch?

- Share how you felt when you got to the end of a project that had meaning to you. How did it make you feel about yourself and your abilities?

- Set next week's homework: Read the chapter, "Developing Your Creativity Further," and do the personal activations.

Developing Your Creativity Further

- Looking back over the tips for developing your creativity, were there any that stood out to this group's members? Why?

- Discuss – In what ways do you find that self-criticism and judgment play a part in how you view your creativity? Do they affect the job you do as you create?

- How do you find that other people's opinions affect your creativity?

STUDY GUIDE QUESTIONS

- Discuss how easy or difficult it is to find time, or give themselves permission, to play and/or pursue creative things. How easy is it to allow themselves to be messy?

- Discuss how much the fear of failure or rejection affects them in their creativity.

- Set next week's homework: Read the chapter, "Creativity in Later Life," and do the personal activations.

Creativity in Later Life

- What are the "generally believed and promoted" ideas concerning older people and creativity?

- How can we either continue to be creative or develop our creativity as we age? Can we expect to be able to be creative?

- What are some ways you could continue to use and develop your creativity as individuals, or as a group?

- What effect did reading the results of the "Study on Creativity and Aging" by Gene Cohen have on the way you now view what your senior years are or will be like?

- Did it change your viewpoint? If so, how will you follow through? What would you change in your life as a result?

- Discuss how it made you feel when you read the stories of older people who had great creative success in their latter years.

- Set next week's homework: Read the chapter, "Developing a Culture of Creativity," and do the personal activations.

Developing a Culture of Creativity

- Discuss the place creativity currently has in your church or group (this is not a judgment time but an honest assessing). Remember, you can't change something until you look at it honestly and come up with ideas that can help change things.

- Discuss the ways in which you can develop a culture and practice of creativity in your church or group.

- What activities or groups could you start in your church to promote creativity within the lives of the church members?

- Discuss how you can use the creative talent within your church to help and encourage the community around you.

- Set next week's homework: Read the chapter, "More Creativity Activators."

More Creativity Activators

- Ask people to share about any activations from this chapter that stood out to them or they would like to try, and why. What was it about those activations that appealed to them?

- Discuss the ways this study has benefitted the people in your group – individually and as a group.

- Discuss – In what way will you change your life to accommodate creativity more?

- What new things are you going to try?

- Take some time to encourage each other in the growth journey you've been on over the past few weeks. Pair people up, or put them in groups of three, and get them to share words

STUDY GUIDE QUESTIONS

of encouragement with each other about the changes they've seen in one another over the course of the study. Pray for each other.

- Thank them for their involvement and think about setting a time to catch up in a month or so to see how they are doing in implementing their creativity.

The Value of Your Values (bonus chapter)

- Discuss how aware you are of the internal values that guide your life.

- What were some values you discovered you had that surprised you, that you hadn't been aware of until you thought about them or until someone pointed them out to you?

- Discuss how your values have changed over your lifetime. Which ones changed and which ones stayed constant?

- Discuss the ways in which your values have played a part in your creative life, in working with others. Have you found it hard when your values have been infringed on? What did you feel? How did you react?

Acknowledgments

You don't have to be perfect to inspire others, just tell your story and let others make of it what they will.

There are some people I'd like to thank who've recognized and helped me foster my creativity along my journey.

My husband Rob has always been my chief encourager when it comes to trying new things. He has always believed in me and encouraged me, and without that encouragement I know I would not be where I am today. Thank you, darling. Thanks, too, to my kids and kids-in-law, Dan and Aimee, Tanya and Phil – you inspire me and challenge me to extend myself and to try new things.

My birth family. Who knew as we grew up together that each of you would be so creative in so many different ways? You continue to show me how to rise above what life throws at us, to not be defined by the past and to keep creativity alive and growing.

Graeme and Kath Packer – Thank you for pushing me into attending my first art workshop, and thanks also to Hugh Brading who took that workshop and encouraged me to pursue art.

Jeanette Bremner – You constantly inspire me and push me to grow in my creativity, and in other areas, too. Thank you for being my dear friend.

Thanks to Patricia King and the XP Publishing Team – Carol Martinez, Steve Fryer, and Lila Nelson. Your belief in me and my creativity and the encouragement and help you've given in getting this book ready for publishing means so much to me.

Of course, my thanks would not be complete without recognizing my biggest fan and champion – the one who gave me my creativity – Father God Himself. I am so thankful for His encouragement and inspiration, and I'm glad that He always has room for my pictures on His fridge and my books in His library!

There are many others who I might have acknowledged but haven't – to you I say "thank you" as well. Much of what I've learned has been gleaned from others along the way. Like a magpie, I've tucked away bits from here and bits from there, and other people's ideas have become mine through use and time. If I have unwittingly included something that you believe to be your idea in this book without acknowledging you, please forgive me, I have tried not to do so.

About Lyn Packer

Dream big dreams, see what may be, then go out and create them. Live those dreams – you can make them your reality, you know. It's never really impossible.

Hi, I'm Lyn Packer, the author of this book.

I love being creative, and I love encouraging others in their creativity, too. But it wasn't always so; because of childhood abuse I had a very "locked within myself" childhood, and my creativity didn't start to blossom until I was in my twenties. But when it did, it opened up a whole new world to me, a lifetime of co-creating with God and ministering creatively to others.

Now I get to express my creativity in many ways – through story, poetry, teaching articles and books, blogs, painting, sculpture, dance, jewelry making, teaching and more. I've published books covering a variety of subjects, and have produced teaching CDs as well. I've taught prophetic dance in several nations. I've held solo art exhibitions and taken part in group exhibitions, even winning prizes in some, and I have taught classes on prophetic art. Yet none of that would ever have happened if I hadn't overcome my many fears and insecurities and given things a go.

And so I get to live this life I love, being creative and helping others to develop their creativity. I get to see them step into the reality of realising and developing their God-given creativity. I watch them have fun in the process and discover that there is far more to them than they know. Now, with this book I get the privilege of encouraging you also. Please do feel free to contact me and share some of your creations and creative experiences. I'd love to hear from you. I can be contacted at the email address below. If you want to find out more about any of my resources, just go to the web store at the website mentioned below.

Website - www.xpnewzealand.com

Email - lpacker@xpministries.com

Facebook Page – @creativepropheticcommunicator

www.ingramcontent.com/pod-product-compliance
Lightning Source LLC
Chambersburg PA
CBHW070102080526
44586CB00013B/1164